MW01351239

The Valuation of Office Properties

A Contemporary Perspective

by Barrett A. Slade, PhD, MAI

Readers of this text may be interested in the following publications from the Appraisal Institute:

- *The Appraisal of Nursing Facilities*
- *The Appraisal of Real Estate*, 13th edition
- *Appraising Industrial Properties*
- *The Dictionary of Real Estate Appraisal*, 4th edition
- *Market Analysis for Real Estate: Concepts and Applications in Valuation and Highest and Best Use*
- *Subdivision Valuation*

Appraisal Institute®
Professionals Providing Real Estate Solutions

The Valuation of Office Properties

A Contemporary Perspective

by Barrett A. Slade, PhD, MAI

Appraisal Institute • 550 West Van Buren • Chicago, IL 60607 • www.appraisalinstitute.org

The Appraisal Institute advances global standards, methodologies, and practices through the professional development of property economics worldwide.

Reviewers: Gail Cooper, MAI
Stephen T. Crosson, MAI, SRA
Don M. Emerson, Jr., MAI, SRA
Richard Marchitelli, MAI

Chief Executive Officer: Frederick H. Grubbe
Director, Communications, Marketing & Member Resources: Hope Atuel
Senior Manager, Publications: Stephanie Shea-Joyce
Senior Technical Writer: Michael McKinley
Technical Book Editor: Emily Ruzich
Manager, Book Design and Production: Michael Landis
Production Specialist: Sandra Williams

Library of Congress Cataloging-in-Publication Data

Slade, Barrett A.
The valuation of office properties : a contemporary perspective / Barrett A. Slade.
p. cm.
Includes bibliographical references.
ISBN 978-1-935328-04-9
1. Office buildings–Valuation–United States. 2. Commercial buildings–Valuation–United States. I. Title.
HD1393.58.U6S55 2009
333.33'8720973--dc22

2009018260

Table of Contents

About the Author

Barrett A. Slade, PhD, MAI, is an associate professor of finance at the Marriott School at Brigham Young University. He received his PhD in real estate from the University of Georgia and holds the MAI designation from the Appraisal Institute. He has over 25 years of experience in the appraisal profession. His experience includes serving as vice president and chief appraiser for the First Interstate Bank of Arizona and as president of Slade and Associates, a real estate appraisal and consulting firm located in the Phoenix metropolitan area. In addition, Mr. Slade's consulting experience includes due diligence investigations, disposition strategies, portfolio valuation, market segmentation analysis, feasibility studies, white paper research studies, problem property strategies, and expert witness testimony. His research has been published in numerous real estate finance and economics journals, including *The Appraisal Journal*, *Real Estate Economics*, the *Journal of Real Estate Finance and Economics*, the *Journal of Real Estate Research*, the *National Tax Journal*, the *Journal of Real Estate Practice and Education*, the *Institutional Real Estate Letter*, *Real Estate Review*, and the *Journal of Real Estate Portfolio Management*.

# Acknowledgments

An undertaking of this magnitude is not accomplished without the assistance of many talented individuals. I wish to gratefully acknowledge the helpful comments and suggestions provided by the reviewers and by Appraisal Institute staff, who provided valuable assistance with the manuscript.

I also wish to express my appreciation to Vincent M. Dowling, MAI, SRA; Stephen D. Roach, MAI; John R. Underwood, Jr., MAI, SRA; and Lee H. Waronker, MAI, SRA who provided helpful comments and suggestions in the development of the Appraisal Institute seminar *Office Building Valuation: A Contemporary Perspective*, which provided the foundation for this manuscript. As the author, however, I assume full responsibility for the final product, including any errors or shortcomings.

Foreword

Valuing office buildings presents a distinct set of challenges to the appraiser. The Appraisal Institute is pleased to present this new text, which offers practical tools to meet these challenges. *The Valuation of Office Properties: A Contemporary Perspective* covers the terminology, concepts, principles, and analytical techniques related to the proper valuation of office buildings, focusing in particular on the income capitalization approach and the complexities of valuing multitenant office properties.

The Valuation of Office Properties begins with an overview of the history of the office building and the characteristic attributes of different types of office buildings. Important issues relating to site and improvement inspection and analysis, including industry measurement criteria, are then addressed. The income capitalization approach is given a thorough examination in Chapter 5, which discusses topics such as office leases, forecasting cash flows, direct and yield capitalization, and estimating rents, vacancies, and operating expenses. An in-depth case study is presented to reinforce these concepts. The concluding chapters explore the sales comparison approach, the cost approach, and final reconciliation as they relate to office building valuation. True-to-life examples are provided throughout the text to illustrate the concepts presented, and a glossary and bibliography are included for further reference.

The Valuation of Office Properties: A Contemporary Perspective provides up-to-date coverage of a unique and exciting field of real estate appraisal. This text will be a valuable tool for beginning appraisers wishing to expand their knowledge and skill set and for more experienced appraisers who want to brush up on the fundamentals of office building appraisal.

Jim Amorin, MAI, SRA
2009 President
Appraisal Institute

Chapter 1

The Origin and History of Office Properties

The origin of the office building and its subsequent history is, unfortunately, not very well documented. Numerous articles and books on the architecture and construction of the office building exist, but little is said about the history and evolution of the office building as an integral part of everyday business. This may be largely attributed to the fact that the construction of office buildings as a distinct land use surfaced only about 100 years ago. As a result, the modern office building may be considered to be one of the significant technological advances of the last century.[1]

The Origin of the Office Building

The term *office* comes from the Latin *officium*, which means "a mobile bureau or human staff." The emergence of the office is closely linked to the businesses of ancient Greece and Rome. In ancient times, offices were located in palaces or temples and housed important documents or scrolls. These areas have often been referred to by historians as "libraries," which may not be entirely accurate since they were most likely intended for record-keeping and management functions.

Record-keeping and management functions were enhanced with the invention of double-entry bookkeeping, which stimulated geographic business centers during the Renaissance. As early as 1480, banking and trading houses began building facilities in financial centers, some of which are still being used today. The town halls of the fourteenth through sixteenth centuries could arguably be considered among the earliest modern office buildings.[2]

---

1. Richard MacCormac, "The Dignity of the Office," *The Architectural Review*, vol. 190, no. 1143 (May 1992): 76; Peggy J. Crawford and John L. Hysom, "The Evolution of Office Building Research," *The Journal of Real Estate Literature* (July 1997).

2. John R. White, ed., *The Office Building: From Concept to Investment Reality* (Chicago: Appraisal Institute, American Society of Real Estate Counselors, and Society of Industrial and Office Realtors, 1993); Cruickshank, Dan, "Origins of Offices," *The Architectural Review* (November 1983).

The Nineteenth Century

The office property became a separate land use in the nineteenth century due to the emergence of special requirements regarding use, planning, and finances.[3] Initial development of the office property was limited by a lack of demand for large amounts of office space and the technology to construct more than a few stories.[4] By the 1830s, however, four- and five-story office buildings began appearing to meet the demand for business space in growing cities. As growth continued, the number of office buildings increased accordingly. The typical office building at this time was usually two to five stories high, 50 feet wide or less, and constructed of brick and mortar. It also usually included a store area, with the office located above the store and accessible by a narrow staircase. These buildings had little fire protection and only the simplest sanitary facilities.

As transportation improved with the development of trains and the Industrial Revolution matured, a major change occurred. Businesses and manufacturing facilities began locating along railroad transportation lines, especially at transfer points. This growth led to increased land prices in the downtown districts, where many of the transfer points were located.

In response to increased land prices and congestion in cities, households began relocating further away from commercial centers, which created even more space for businesses and government agencies to build offices close to commercial centers. The creation of a downtown area resulted from this growth, and new office construction continued in city areas for nearly a century.[5]

In addition to improved transportation, key inventions helped spur the evolution and development of the office. The first of these were gaslights and electric light. Lighting homes with gaslights was essentially unknown prior to the nineteenth century, and it was not until the mid-nineteenth century that gas lighting became widespread. Joseph Swan and Thomas Edison invented electric light in 1878 and 1879, respectively. Although their invention did not fare well initially, electric lights found their way into homes and office buildings, eventually replacing gaslights in most communities.[6]

The invention of the flushing toilet in the nineteenth century allowed for indoor restrooms. (Prior to that time, outdoor outhouses were used.) Also, Alexander Cumming's invention of the sink trap ultimately allowed office tenants to enjoy the convenient use of restrooms in office buildings without having to deal with the waste.[7]

---

3. Cruickshank, "Origins of Offices."
4. Crawford and Hysom, "The Evolution of Office Building Research."
5. White, *The Office Building*.
6. Charles Panati, *Panati's Browser's Book of Beginnings* (Boston: Houghton Mifflin, 1984).
7. Charles Panati, *Panati's Extraordinary Origins of Everyday Things* (New York: Harper & Row, 1987).

The invention of the passenger elevator also promoted the development of the office. Before the passenger elevator, the market value of office space declined as its distance from the street increased due to the inability or unwillingness of most people to climb higher than five or six floors. Additionally, the incremental revenue received from building additional stories was less than the incremental cost of construction, so most office buildings remained four to six stories high until the late 1800s.[8]

Although passenger elevators were used as early as 1823, they were not widely used because they were not safe enough to transport people at relatively fast speeds. In 1852, Elisha Graves Otis overcame this problem by developing a safety brake-equipped, steam-driven passenger elevator. The first elevator of this design was installed in a five-story building in 1857. Design improvements soon allowed similarly equipped elevators to reach heights of 10 to 12 stories, and by 1898 such an elevator could reach 30 stories. About 20 years after Otis developed the safety brake for the passenger elevator, C. W. Baldwin of the Otis Company invented the geared hydraulic elevator. As a result, buildings could be even taller. Passenger elevators became an essential part of the office building, increasing the rents of higher floors, which were now more desirable because they were far above the noise and dust of the street.[9]

The introduction of skeleton construction further promoted the development of office buildings. In the 1840s, Daniel Badger and James Bogardus introduced the use of cast-iron and glass buildings, which quickly gained widespread popularity. The use of iron in facades provided more light for the ever-growing office building because the slender cast-iron frame allowed builders to reduce the width of walls between windows. The use of cast-iron construction, however, was quickly abandoned following major citywide fires in Chicago, New York, and Boston, which collectively demonstrated that it was not the best material available. Office building developers then turned to the use of steel embedded in concrete.[10]

The introduction of the steel superstructure, coupled with the passenger elevator, made tall buildings possible as well as more practical. In 1885, Chicago's Home Insurance Building–a tall building with a skeleton frame designed by architect William LeBaron Jenney–was constructed. This is considered by some historians to be the first skyscraper.[11] The office building, once limited in height because of inconvenience and inadequate building technology, began to take on a new form.

Following the 1871 Chicago fire, a number of technological developments emerged to improve the soundness of the office building. Fireproofing was introduced in 1880, foundations became more reliable

8. "History of Offices and Clerical Labor: Early Office Buildings," Early Office Museum Web site, *http://www.officemuseum.com/office_buildings.htm*; White, *The Office Building*.

9. Ibid.

10. Cruickshank, "Origins of Offices;" White, *The Office Building*.

11. Cruickshank, "Origins of Offices."

around 1885, and self-supporting steel-frame construction became popular around 1890, all of which led to tremendous growth in the size, number, and location of office buildings.[12]

Downtown land prices continued to increase during this time, making taller buildings more profitable as inner-city employment grew and companies vied for central city locations. The tallest office buildings were found in the largest American cities, such as New York and Chicago, where central city land prices were the highest.[13]

The Twentieth Century

Between 1880 and 1920, an intense period of office building growth resulted from increases in

- The height, size, and number of office buildings
- The number of office workers, particularly clerical workers
- The number of female workers (in clerical positions)
- The use of specialized office machines and office products[14]

This growth was further supported by improved roads and automobiles as well as steam-powered rapid transit lines, which brought employees and workers in from areas outside the central city.

Prominent businesses began designing buildings to demonstrate their wealth and power. The earliest and best-known examples of this phenomenon are office buildings erected by large insurance companies. These centrally located buildings were strategically located to be accessible via main transit lines and convenient to clients and employees.[15] They also offered impressive views and were light and airy, easily cleaned, and attractive.

The office building boom that characterized the first two decades of the 1900s came to a standstill with the onset of the Great Depression. Although a few major office structures were built during this time, new construction did not resume in earnest until the end of World War II in 1945. Demand for office space increased as those who had fought in the war returned home, looking for employment. Because available space was in short supply and demand was high, rents increased to new levels.

Advances during the years following World War II contributed to another boom in office building construction. Passenger elevators could now carry passengers up or down 30 stories in less than 60 seconds. Office layouts changed and improved with the introduction of central

12. "History of Offices and Clerical Labor: Early Office Buildings," Early Office Museum Web site; Crawford and Hysom, "The Evolution of Office Building Research;" Cruickshank, "Origins of Offices."

13. "History of Offices and Clerical Labor: Early Office Buildings," Early Office Museum Web site.

14. Ibid.

15. White, *The Office Building*.

air conditioning. Stoker-fired coal boilers were replaced with oil and gas boilers, which were soon followed by electric heating. New floor coverings emerged, and steel and reinforced concrete became major structural materials.[16]

At around the time of the Eisenhower administration (1953–1961), suburban communities wanting for revenues lured office development to the suburbs through liberal zoning laws and other incentives. Decay in the downtown areas of cities also encouraged businesses to relocate to the suburbs. As a result, construction of office buildings increased in suburban areas, with suburban development soon outpacing urban development.[17]

During the 1960s, central air conditioning became an office building standard, and floor plans became more flexible as a result. Ceiling heights were reduced to eight feet in many buildings with air conditioning, yet remained at nine feet or higher in Class A office buildings. Additionally, floor-to-ceiling windows and electric heating systems became common. As computer and communications technology advanced, *smart buildings* began to be constructed. These buildings were prewired for computer networks, and the structures were made to hold increasing amounts of wiring. Smart buildings also demonstrated a higher level of technological capacity in their heating, cooling, and ventilation systems. By the 1980s, specially designed computer rooms were included in most new office buildings to support increasing computer needs.

In the 1980s, new issues affected office buildings. The air supplied by central heating and air conditioning systems allowed toxic substances and germs to accumulate, leading to *sick building syndrome*.[18] These problems, however, did not slow construction. The growing number of white-collar jobs, accompanied by the increased availability of mortgage money for construction resulting from increased tax advantages for commercial construction, led to yet another office building boom.[19]

The Twenty-First Century

Robust growth in the office sector has continued into the twenty-first century. This may be, in large part, a result of continued growth in the service sector. Presently, technological advances occur on a daily basis and firms are becoming more global in orientation. Only time will tell what office buildings will look like in the future and what their status in society will be. However, the office building currently maintains a significant presence in the urban landscape and is an integral part of the global economy as well as our daily lives.

16. Ibid.

17. "History of Offices and Clerical Labor: Early Office Buildings," Early Office Museum Web site.

18. White, *The Office Building*.

19. Crawford and Hysom, "The Evolution of Office Building Research."

Chapter 2

Types of Office Buildings and Valuation Nuances

Less-experienced appraisers tend to view office properties as a homogeneous product with little differentiation. A closer examination, however, reveals that there are many types of office properties, each with unique valuation nuances that must be carefully examined in order to render a reliable estimate of their value. Some of the office building types that an appraiser might encounter include the following:

- Low-rise, single-tenant
- Low-rise, multitenant
- Mid-rise (4 to 16 stories)
- High-rise (16 or more stories)
- Office with street-level retail space
- Medical or dental office
- Office condominium
- Bank branch
- Veterinary hospital or clinic
- Office with retail and residential space

This list is not necessarily complete, but it does illustrate the diversity in the office sector. Because of the role that property type plays in the valuation process, it is vital that the appraiser understand the valuation nuances of the most common types of office properties. This discussion is not intended to be comprehensive but rather to assist the appraiser in learning how to critically examine each office property and its unique characteristics.

Low-Rise, Single-Tenant Office Building

A low-rise, single-tenant office property, such as the one shown in the accompanying photo, is designed to accommodate one firm. Note that *low-rise* refers to a building that is one to three stories high. When an appraiser encounters a low-rise, single-tenant office building in a valuation assignment, it is important to first determine if the property truly

A low-rise, single-tenant office building

is a single-tenant office property or an office property that could accommodate multiple tenants but is presently occupied by only one. This can be done by examining the building design and determining if it restricts the building's use to one occupant or firm. In reality, many so-called single-tenant buildings can actually accommodate multiple tenants but are presently occupied by just one. If it is determined that only one firm can occupy the building–i.e., it truly is a single-tenant building–then proper investigation of functional obsolescence is critical.

Functional obsolescence frequently occurs because of the thin market conditions that true single-tenant properties encounter as a result of building size. In other words, finding a tenant of the right size as well as the right type may be very difficult. Many potential tenants may like the location of the space and its general design attributes but may need more or less space than the building actually offers. In fact, for true single-tenant properties, rents on a per-square-foot basis are frequently lower than those of similar multitenant buildings. This happens because tenants in single-tenant offices essentially agree to occupy more space than they actually need, and therefore negotiate lower rents. Of course, the reverse may be true in some markets. For instance, a well-designed, free-standing, single-tenant office building may have considerably more appeal than a nearby multitenant office building because of unique visibility and signage as well as superior quality of construction and custom finishes. It is important that the appraiser investigate this issue for the subject property to determine if the building suffers from this common form of obsolescence or enjoys a comparative advantage that may be unique to the single-tenant design.

Single-tenant office buildings are generally found in suburban locations where land values are lower than values in urban locations. The buyers of single-tenant office buildings are typically individuals or small partnerships or corporations that have a higher cost of capital than institutional investors. Therefore, higher capitalization and discount rates are sometimes observed for these types of properties. In addition, single-tenant or single-occupant buildings are frequently occupied by the owners, who provide no rent history. As a result, the appraiser must rely entirely on a market rent study to estimate the market rental rate for the subject property rather than also considering the existing rent roll and operating history often available for multitenant properties.

2) Low-Rise, Multitenant Office Building

Low-rise (one to three stories), multitenant office properties are the most common type of office property that appraisers encounter. The low-rise, multitenant office is typically located in the suburbs. Similar to single-tenant, low-rise properties, this type of property is generally bought by individuals or small partnerships or corporations. As noted with single-tenant office properties, capitalization rates and discount rates may be higher than those of larger office properties due to higher costs of capital encountered by the typical buyer of this property type. higher rates

Because of the building's multitenant design, the ability to reconfigure the space to accommodate varying tenant sizes is critical when determining the functionality of a low-rise, multitenant office building. Designs that allow for greater flexibility are considered more functional, and greater functionality leads to greater rental income.

Tenant mix is another important attribute that must be considered by the appraiser. The tenant mix may be synergistic and result in above-market rents or detrimental and result in below-market rents. If tenants are highly compatible and benefit directly from their proximity to each other, then the tenants may be willing to pay a premium to continue residing in the building. synergistic For example, an appraiser who leases office space in a building that is also occupied by a title company (which may provide data access), a large commercial real estate brokerage firm (which may provide business opportunities and data access), a commercial mortgage

A low-rise, multitenant office building

lender (which may provide business opportunities), and a law firm that specializes in real estate (more business opportunities) may be willing to pay a rent premium because of these business benefits.

The opposite situation may also be found when firms have virtually no synergistic relationship and are negatively impacted by other tenants. An example of this is a telemarketing firm that divides its space into hundreds of cubicles, resulting in virtually no parking availability for the building's other tenants. A careful property inspection will frequently uncover these types of important valuation issues.

Mid-Rise Office Building

Mid-rise office buildings are diverse in design and location. Mid-rise buildings can be found in the central business district (CBD) of a city or the suburbs. Of course, high-rise properties tend to be located in or near the CBD, while low-rise properties tend to be located in the suburbs. The story height of mid-rise office buildings may vary but typically falls between four and 16 stories. As the story height increases, so does the construction cost per unit. In addition, architectural complexities increase with story height due to safety and regulatory requirements, such as fire codes.

The capacity and quality of the building's systems are very important to tenants and are reflected in the building's rents and occupancy rates. Some of these systems include the transportation systems (elevators and stairwells), ventilation systems (quality of air filtration and heating and cooling zones), and technology systems (high-capacity Internet and

A mid-rise office building

telephone). It is vital that the appraiser adequately assess the capacity, quality, and condition of the various building systems and compare these characteristics with similar, competing buildings to determine the subject property's competitive position in the marketplace.

While still focusing on the physical characteristics of the building, it is important that the appraiser also assess the design and functionality of the building floor plates–i.e., the layout of the horizontal space on each floor. Generally, the floor plate for each story is similar because of vertical penetrations (elevator shafts, stairwells, and ventilation shafts) and load-bearing columns. Functionally designed floor plates allow for more flexibility and alternative build-out configurations, provide better proximity to elevators and restrooms, and maximize any view amenities the building may have.

The adequacy and location of parking are other important considerations in valuing office properties. Parking may be an even greater issue for mid-rise and high-rise properties because higher rents are required to justify the costs of vertical construction. In other words, tenants that pay high rents expect good parking in terms of both adequacy and proximity to the elevator bays. A mid-rise building may have many positive characteristics, but if the parking attributes are viewed negatively, the entire building can suffer.

The tenant profile for a mid-rise office building often differs depending on the location of the property. For mid-rise properties in the suburbs, the tenant is frequently a local firm that desires higher visibility in the local market. Tenants frequently vacate low-rise properties to occupy mid-rise properties. As a result, the absorption of space in a new mid-rise property in the suburbs generally comes from low-rise, multitenant properties in the immediate vicinity.

For mid-rise properties located in the CBD, however, the tenant is frequently a national firm that requires a CBD location but does not necessarily require the premium locations provided by the trophy properties. When appraising a proposed mid-rise office building in the suburbs, it is imperative that the appraiser properly assess the strength of the local office market in terms of both occupancy and rental rates. A large, new, speculative mid-rise office property in the suburbs may create oversupply conditions because the local market may not be substantial enough to absorb the new space. Therefore, appraisers must be very careful when appraising a new or proposed mid-rise property in the suburbs.

4) High-Rise Office Building

High-rise office buildings are at least sixteen stories high and typically located in a CBD, where the location generates rents that are high enough to justify high construction costs and land prices. The tenant profile generally includes a national credit tenant or prestigious local firm that demands high visibility and excellent proximity to other firms.

A high-rise office building

A high-rise property is often referred to as a "signature building" because some of its premium space is usually occupied by a large national credit tenant who places identifying signage on the property.

As in mid-rise properties, important building attributes in high-rise buildings include transportation, ventilation, and technology systems as well as floor plate design, parking, and transportation. One particular aspect of high-rise buildings that must be carefully examined is any possible view amenity. Rental rates may vary considerably depending on the story height and the particular view offered. In existing office properties, the view amenity may be clearly identified in the existing leases; however, for new or proposed high-rise properties, estimating the market rental rates may require careful examination of the view amenity.

Buyers and owners of high-rise properties are typically institutional investors such as insurance companies and pension funds. The cost of capital for these owners is generally lower than the cost of capital for smaller companies, which may influence the capitalization rate, the discount rate, or both.

Office Building with Street-Level Retail

Office properties that offer street-level retail are typically located in the CBD or areas with high levels of foot traffic. The retail tenants generally consist of restaurants, copy centers, bookstores, coffee shops, souvenir stores, or other similar, smaller tenants that offer a service to occupants of the office space or draw clientele from the foot traffic generated by nearby businesses or tourist attractions. Visibility is essential for the retail tenants, so design and street presentation as well as access are important factors that impact rental rates and property values.

Retail tenants generally require specialized tenant improvements that are more costly than common office space, and this must, of course, be factored into the analysis. In addition, the lease structures for retail tenants often vary from the lease structures for office tenants. For instance, retail tenants may have a net lease or may be required to pay a base rent as well as a percentage of their retail sales, whereas the office tenants may have a full-service (gross) lease with an expense stop. In short, the varying lease structures and tenant improvements require more market research and add to the complexity of the appraisal assignment.

If a restaurant tenant is located in the building, it is important to determine its impact on overall building performance. This issue is important because parking can often be negatively impacted during peak times of the day (i.e., lunch and dinner). In addition, noxious odors from the restaurant may infiltrate the office space, creating a negative externality for the office tenants. This may, in turn, negatively impact occupancy and rental income.

Medical or Dental Office Building

Medical and dental office properties tend to be located in the suburbs near residential developments, providing better proximity for patients. They also tend to cluster near hospitals and other medical facilities.

An office building with street-level retail area

Significant technological changes have occurred over the last 10 to 20 years, frequently creating a "renovate or build new" dilemma for many older hospitals. Hospitals frequently elect to build new facilities in different locations rather than renovate. New medical office space tends to be built near the new hospital, causing a migration from the old office space located near the old hospital. This type of scenario can have a devastating impact on the older medical office space in the form of high vacancies. Therefore, the appraiser must perform a proper market analysis to investigate this possibility and the impact that this potential problem may have on the value of the subject property.

One distinct characteristic of medical and dental office space is the additional cost of tenant improvements due to specialized plumbing and electrical requirements. Additionally, the parking ratios for medical and dental office properties are generally higher than those for other office properties due to the higher intensity of use (i.e., the typically large numbers of patients). On a positive note, medical and dental tenants tend to be very stable, long-term occupants because of their investment in tenant improvements as well as the nature of medical practices. In short, they find it hard to move. The stability of rental income and the creditworthiness of the tenants may result in less risk to the forecast cash flows, leading to higher values.

It is also important to note that hospitals frequently offer medical office space to physicians at below-market rates to induce doctors to practice at their hospitals. This favorable rent structure may exert competitive pressure on nearby medical office properties that are not owned by hospitals.

A medical/dental office building

Office Condominium Building

Office condominiums have a legal ownership structure similar to that of residential condominiums. Each individual unit has a separate legal description, and an owners association oversees the common area. Office condominiums are located in both CBD and suburban markets but are usually found in the suburbs in low-rise properties. Small business owners with stable employment growth are attracted to office condominiums due to the advantages of ownership over leasing, such as equity build-up.

Appraisers may be asked to appraise a single unit for an individual owner or an entire condominium complex as proposed construction. The appraisal of an individual unit is similar to that of a single-tenant office property, while the appraisal of a condominium complex is similar to that of a sell-out property such as a residential subdivision. In the second case, the objective is to first estimate the retail value of each individual unit as well as the absorption and selling expenses; the estimated cash flows are then discounted at a market discount rate to estimate the present value of all the units as of the valuation date.

For both existing and proposed construction, the owners association budget is a very important item that requires careful examination. If the association budget is insufficient, then inadequate maintenance will occur, resulting in a decline in property value. On the other hand, a very liberal budget results in good property care but decreases the cash flow available for the property. In short, most owners associations struggle to find the "right" budget, which provides for adequate care and maintenance but does not overtax the cash flow. Because office condominiums are becoming more popular, appraisers are encountering these valuation assignments more often.

An office condominium building

Bank Branch Building

A bank branch is usually located on the ground floor of a signature high-rise office building in a CBD or on a stand-alone pad site in the suburbs. (A *pad site* is an improved site that is typically part of a larger retail shopping complex but allows for a free-standing building, such as a fast-food restaurant.) Banks and other types of financial institutions typically want to convey a successful image, so they generally occupy premium locations and have high-end tenant improvements such as marble floors and mahogany paneling. High-end security features such as vaults and security systems also result in higher tenant improvement costs compared to those of general office spaces.

Stand-alone bank branches located on pad sites are typically designed for single-tenant occupancy, which must be adequately addressed if the property is no longer going to be used as a bank branch. Because of the premium locations that older bank branches frequently occupy, a careful highest and best use analysis may be required.

Veterinary Hospital or Clinic Building

Veterinarians have recently been locating small animal practices in multitenant buildings. Appraisers must be careful to examine the potential detrimental impact that this use has on other tenants. Unique sounds and smells are associated with veterinary practices. Buildings that house stand-alone veterinary clinics and feature unique designs and configurations may be considered special-purpose properties, requiring broader market research of comparable data.

Veterinary clinics are generally located in the suburbs near residential subdivisions for easy patient access. Like general medical office space, veterinary clinics have high tenant improvement expenses due to spe-

A bank branch building

A veterinary hospital/clinic building

cialized plumbing and electrical requirements. In addition, the parking ratios can be higher than those of standard office spaces.

Office/Retail/Residential Building

Appraisals of multiuse properties, like the one shown on page 18, are some of the more complex and difficult appraisal assignments in the office property domain. These properties are almost always located in the CBD, where there is adequate demand for their varying uses. The complexity in the appraisal assignment results from the varying lease structures created by the different types of tenants. For instance, the office leases may be full-service with an expense stop, the retail leases may be absolute net with a percentage clause, and the residential leases may be gross except for the payment of utilities. Each lease type may exhibit different terms. In addition, the diversity in tenant types may make risk assessment more challenging. In short, more market research is required by the appraiser to reliably estimate property value.

A multiuse office/retail/residential building

Chapter

3 Site Analysis

The physical and legal characteristics of a site can have a significant impact on the value of an office property; therefore, a separate analysis of site characteristics must be carefully performed.

Preparing for the Inspection

The first step in the site analysis is to prepare for the inspection. This is accomplished by compiling all relevant data that may be readily available from the client, public records, and third-party data providers such as title companies. These items may include a copy of the site plan and survey from the property owner or client, location maps, county plat maps, Federal Emergency Management Agency (FEMA) flood maps, zoning maps, neighborhood maps, traffic maps, aerial maps, topographical maps, assessor's property data, and community profiles, just to name a few.

In preparation for the on-site inspection, the appraiser packs a camera and relevant measuring instruments and then contacts the client and arranges for an on-site inspection. If possible, the client is invited to attend the inspection to answer questions and ensure that important property information is not inadvertently overlooked.

Assembling, Verifying, and Analyzing the Facts

Location

The formal address (including the street number, street name, city, state, and zip code) is verified by comparing it to relevant documents such as an assessor's tax notice. In addition, the legal description is verified from a title report or an ownership conveyance document such as a deed. The legal description is sometimes noted on the building plans. It is important to ensure that this legal description is consistent with a title report or conveying document. Typically, the plat map or site plan corresponds with the formal legal description found in the title report. Any discrepancies must be investigated and noted in the appraisal report.

An unresolved discrepancy in the legal description may result in an unreliable appraisal, so discrepancies must be resolved with the client prior to continuing with the appraisal. If the appraiser must make an assumption regarding the probable location of the property boundaries, then he or she should clearly articulate this *extraordinary assumption* in the appraisal report.

Area and Shape

Assuming that the legal description has been verified and found to be consistent with the recorded plat map or development site plan, the area and shape of the site must be clearly delineated in the report. A copy of the plat map or site plan best illustrates the shape and boundaries of the site, although a narrative description may enhance the illustration. For office properties, the area of the site is typically reported in both square feet and acres. Next, the appraiser must examine and establish the level of functionality and marketability of the site. For instance, the size and shape of the site may severely limit its development potential, thereby reducing its market acceptance.

Public Utilities

The availability and adequacy of necessary public utilities is critical for contemporary office properties. These include the following:

- Drinking water
- Sanitary sewer
- Electricity
- Natural gas
- Telephone
- High-speed Internet
- Cable television

The appraiser generally identifies the location, availability, and capacity of each of these utilities by examining local utility maps. If utility maps are not readily available, the appraiser must contact each of the respective utility companies to verify the location and capacity of the utility lines. A brief conversation with the owner or client regarding the availability of the utilities is typically not enough to ensure adequate due diligence, especially for vacant land that is being considered for office development.

Once the factual data is obtained, the appraiser analyzes the impact of the utilities on the marketability or value of the property. For instance, high-speed Internet is considered a necessity in modern business. Therefore, a lack of access to high-speed capability would negatively impact the lease rates and marketability of the property, resulting in a decrease in market value.

Street Improvements

Office properties are commonly located on major arterial streets that are both easily accessible and visible. During the inspection, the appraiser should examine the off-site improvements that are adjacent to the site, including the street surface, curbs, gutters, sidewalks, streetlights, and landscaping. The level and condition of these improvements influence the subject property's competitive position in the market and must be reported and considered in the valuation process.

Soil and Subsoil Conditions

When speaking of soil and subsoil conditions, the focus is not on the agricultural capacity of the soil but on any characteristics that might limit or restrict building improvements on the site. For instance, the load-bearing capacity of the soil may limit the size and height of the building. This can also be true for subsoil conditions, such as a high water table. Overcoming inadequate soil or subsoil conditions may be prohibitively expensive, severely limiting the development potential of the property. For existing buildings, this issue has probably been addressed; for proposed projects, however, this issue must be carefully examined.

During the inspection, the appraiser must be attentive to settlement cracks in the floor or wall systems of the building. These may be the first signs of physical deterioration resulting from detrimental soil or subsoil conditions. Appraisers are not trained to assess soil or subsoil conditions, but engineering reports may be available from public sources or from the owner or client. In any case, the appraiser is obligated to disclose any obvious signs of soil or subsoil problems in the report. A special limiting condition may be necessary to alert the client to a potential problem and to clearly identify any related assumptions the appraiser makes in the valuation process.

Topography, Groundwater, and Vegetation

The topography of the site can be determined from topographical maps as well as the on-site inspection. In some cases, hilly topography may provide excellent views and visibility, resulting in rent premiums; however, these premiums may be offset by increased development costs. This important relationship may be examined by conducting market rent surveys and investigating the unique development costs resulting from the topographical conditions. Extreme topographical conditions are typically more favorable for residential rather than commercial construction because of limited access and the low-density regulatory requirements often encountered in these areas.

Similarly, adverse groundwater conditions may severely restrict development opportunities by imposing costly abatement requirements. Appraisers are not trained to determine groundwater conditions or assess the alternatives and costs required to overcome any adverse conditions. However, a careful check of publicly available hydrology reports or water table charts may be required if this is a known problem in the area. For a proposed office property, it is imperative that the appraiser ask the client, contractor, or engineer about the groundwater conditions and report the findings in the appraisal document. It is also prudent to include a limiting condition in the report explaining that the appraiser is not qualified to assess groundwater conditions and any adverse groundwater conditions unknown to the appraiser may impact the value conclusion.

The type and level of vegetation on the site may influence the attractiveness and maintenance costs of the property. Although not a significant issue in the valuation process, attractive and properly maintained landscaping enhances the marketability of the property and impacts market rental rates. For the most part, office property owners recognize the importance of curb appeal and hire professional landscaping companies to maintain the property.

Floodplain and FEMA Flood Zones

The possibility of flooding may influence property value negatively. Appraisers must evaluate the floodplain status of the property and lenders must properly assess risk. Lenders may require that the borrower pay for flood insurance if the property is located in a special flood hazard area. Flood hazard areas or flood zones are identified by FEMA, which also administers the National Flood Insurance Program (NFIP).

FEMA's analysis of floodplains in more than 20,400 communities in the United States influences city building regulations and is the basis for insurance activities and mitigation under the NFIP. Flood zones are geographic areas that FEMA has defined according to varying levels of flood risk.[1] Flood zones can be found on a municipality Flood Insurance Rate Map (FIRM), which can be easily accessed using FEMA's online Map Service Center (MSC). Each zone is described by the severity or type of flooding experienced or possible in the area due to its floodplain conditions. The flood zones are split into three risk areas: moderate to low, high, and undetermined, as shown in Exhibit 3.1.

Flood zones are clearly labeled in FIRMs. FIRMs also include a legend explaining the different zones to assist people who are unfamiliar with the FEMA system. Exhibit 3.2 is an example of a FEMA flood zone map.

Ingress and Egress

A functional and well-located office site typically has good ingress and egress from an arterial street. The appraiser's responsibility is to assess the adequacy of this site characteristic. This requires that the appraiser examine a number of factors, including the number of lanes (capacity), the level of traffic congestion near or adjacent to the site, and the location and number of curb cuts, turn lanes, and traffic lights. A traffic-impact study prepared by a qualified engineer may be available to assist the

1. FEMA Web site, *http://msc.fema.gov.*

Exhibit 3.1 **Definitions of FEMA Flood Zone Designations**

Risk	Zone	Description	Flood Ins. Required
Moderate to Low Risk	B, C, and X	Areas outside the 1-percent annual chance floodplain, areas of 1% annual chance sheet flow flooding where average depths are less than 1 foot, areas of 1% annual chance stream flooding where the contributing drainage area is less than 1 square mile, or areas protected from the 1% annual chance flood by levees. No base flood elevations or depths are shown within this zone. Insurance purchase is not required in these zones.	No
High Risk Areas	A	Areas with a 1% annual chance of flooding and a 26% chance of flooding over the life of a 30-year mortgage. Because detailed analyses are not performed for such areas, no depths or base flood elevations are shown within these zones.	Yes
	AE, A1-A30	Areas with a 1% annual chance of flooding and a 26% chance of flooding over the life of a 30-year mortgage. In most instances, base flood elevations derived from detailed analyses are shown at selected intervals within these zones.	
	AH	Areas with a 1% annual chance of shallow flooding, usually in the form of a pond, with an average depth ranging from 1 to 3 feet. These areas have a 26% chance of flooding over the life of a 30-year mortgage. Base flood elevations derived from detailed analyses are shown at selected intervals within these zones.	
	AO	River or stream flood hazard areas and areas with a 1% or greater chance of shallow flooding each year, usually in the form of sheet flow, with an average depth ranging from 1 to 3 feet. These areas have a 26% chance of flooding over the life of a 30-year mortgage. Average flood depths derived from detailed analyses are shown within these zones.	
	AR	Areas with a temporarily increased flood risk due to the building or restoration of a flood control system (such as a levee or a dam). Mandatory flood insurance purchase requirements will apply, but rates will not exceed the rates for unnumbered A zones if the structure is built or restored in compliance with Zone AR floodplain management regulations.	
	A99	Areas with a 1% annual chance of flooding that will be protected by a federal flood control system where construction has reached specified legal requirements. No depths or base flood elevations are shown within these zones.	
High Risk - Coastal Areas	V	Coastal areas with a 1% or greater chance of flooding and an additional hazard associated with storm waves. These areas have a 26% chance of flooding over the life of a 30-year mortgage. No base flood elevations are shown within these zones.	Yes
	VE, V1 - 30	Coastal areas with a 1% or greater chance of flooding and an additional hazard associated with storm waves. These areas have a 26% chance of flooding over the life of a 30-year mortgage. Base flood elevations derived from detailed analyses are shown at selected intervals within these zones.	
Undetermined Risk Areas	D	Areas with possible but undetermined flood hazards. No flood hazard analysis has been conducted. Flood insurance rates are commensurate with the uncertainty of the flood risk.	

Source: Definitions supplied by FEMA, *http://msc.fema.gov*.

Exhibit 3.2 Sample Flood Zone Map

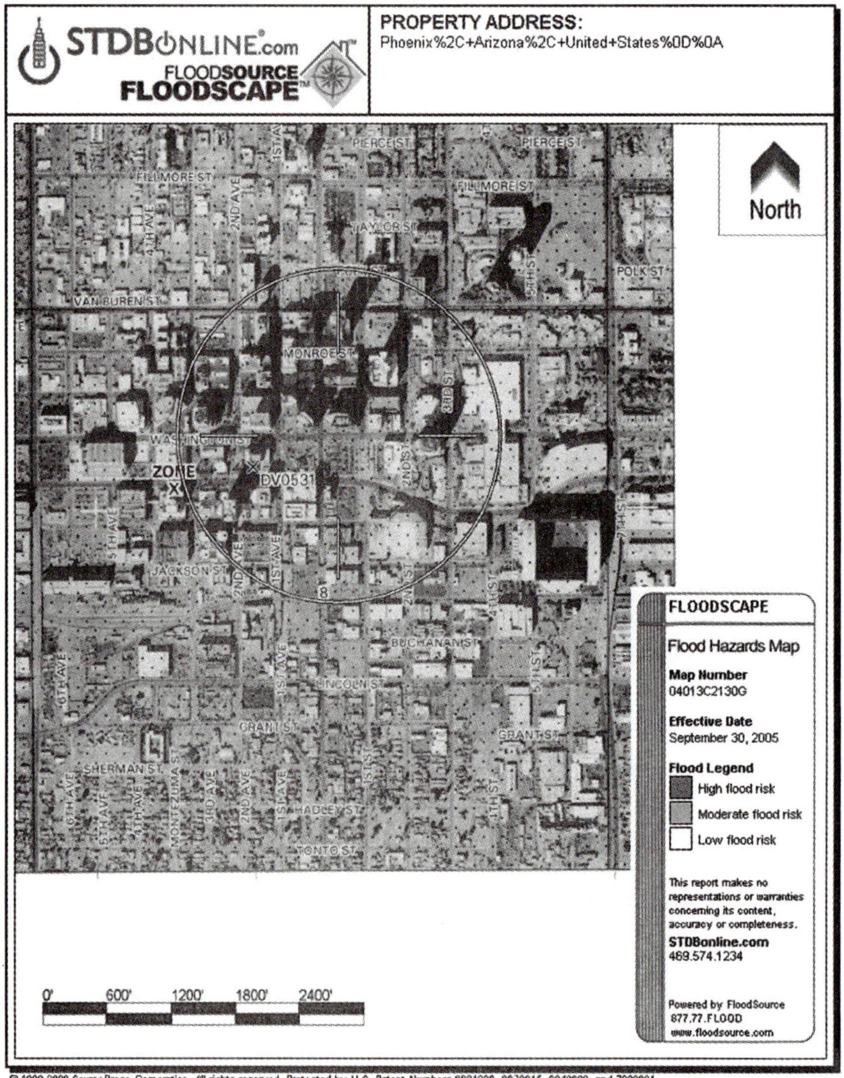

Source: Site To Do Business Web site, *www.stdbonline.com*. Used with permission.

appraiser in this determination. These characteristics are very important to prospective tenants and directly impact rental rates.

Visibility

The visibility of the site is closely aligned with the site's ingress and egress and is determined qualitatively. Proximity to the street, number of traffic lanes, building placement on the site, obstructions, and architecture all influence the visibility of the office property. Visibility is important to office tenants, especially those that desire Class A space.

Frontage-to-Depth Ratio

The site's frontage-to-depth ratio provides a measure of functionality. A very narrow site may negatively influence ingress and egress as well as visibility. In addition, the floor plan may be suboptimal and suffer from functional obsolescence. Conversely, a site with significant frontage and minimal depth may have great visibility but exhibit obsolescence from a poor floor plan, an inadequate parking configuration, or both.

Parking

The configuration of the site tends to influence the parking lot (structure) design. In addition, it may influence the proximity of parking to the building entrances. Tenants are very sensitive to parking adequacy, layout, and proximity to the building. The adequacy of parking may be assessed quantitatively by examining typical parking ratios of competing properties and investigating the municipal parking requirements in the zoning ordinance. The ratios are generally stated as the number of stalls per 1,000 square feet of rentable building area. Low ratios indicate inadequate parking, while high ratios may indicate excess capacity (functional obsolescence due to a superadequacy).

The layout of the parking lot or parking structure directly influences the circulation and ease of ingress and egress. This issue is typically not as critical for office properties as it is for large retail developments, but a clear bottleneck or problematic circulation pattern may negatively influence the rental income of any office property. The location or proximity of the parking lot is probably second in importance to the adequacy of the parking. Prospective tenants respond positively when lots are in close proximity to building entrances with clearly marked walkways and adequate lighting and security. Conversely, distant parking structures with poor lighting and security may negatively influence prospective tenants.

Access to nearby commercial parking garages may actually reduce the on-site parking requirements for downtown office properties. The adequacy and proximity to public transportation systems may also influence the level of on-site parking. The impact of these ancillary parking and transportation alternatives must be assessed by the appraiser and adequately addressed in the valuation process.

Public Restrictions

Zoning typically determines legal activities and building codes. Allowable activities are typically the first aspect of a particular zoning ordinance and determine the intensity of site use. There are various grades of office use, ranging from low-rise garden office space to high-rise office/retail/residential space. The intensity of development is typically governed by building setback, bulk, and height restrictions. Setback and bulk restrictions may limit the building footprint, which may influence the functionality of the space. In addition to height restrictions based on zoning regulations, the Federal Aviation Administration (FAA) may impose further height restrictions, particularly if the property is in a flight path. The building height may also be influenced by "break points" set by the municipality. Break points are typically determined by the fire department's vertical extension capabilities. Proposed construction that exceeds the break points must include greater fire-safety capabilities, which may result in costly construction.

Size and height restrictions for office space are typically embodied in the floor area ratio (FAR). The floor area ratio is defined as "the relationship between the above-ground floor area of a building, as described by the building code, and the area of the plot on which it stands." In planning and zoning, FAR is often expressed as a decimal. For example, a ratio of 2.0 indicates that the permissible floor area of a building is twice the total land area.[2] Exhibit 3.3 provides a conceptual illustration of floor area ratios.

Exhibit 3.3 illustrates an FAR of 1.0 because the site area and building area are equal. Conceptually, the entire site could be covered with one floor, one-half of the site could be covered with two floors, one-fourth of the site could be covered with four floors, and so on. It is important to recognize that the FAR determines the total building area on the site. Once the total building area is calculated, the optimal number of floors can be determined by identifying the ideal floor plate. In other words, market analysis should provide the developer with an indication of floor plate preference. Once the ideal floor plate is identified, the number of floors is calculated by dividing the total building area by the square footage of the ideal floor plate. For benchmarking purposes, FARs for suburban office developments typically fall between 0.25 and 0.50. In urban centers, FARs may be 2.0 to 10.0 or greater.[3]

Private Restrictions

Office property sites may be encumbered by deed restrictions, encroachments, easements, or conditions, covenants, and restrictions (CC&Rs). Typically, a title report or American Land Title Association (ALTA) survey discloses the restrictions that may impact property value. Deed restrictions often limit the future use of the site and are placed in the public records by a previous owner. Onerous deed restrictions may completely modify the highest and best use of the site by restricting all future uses. For example, a deed restriction may limit the site to residential development even though market data suggests that a commercial use would result in greater property value. CC&Rs may exist if the subject site is located in a planned development. CC&Rs generally enhance value by restricting the negative uses on a site. In addition, CC&Rs provide the legal mechanism that allows for the collection of fees that pay for com-

---

2. *The Dictionary of Real Estate Appraisal*, 4th ed. (Chicago: Appraisal Institute, 2002).
3. John R. White, ed., *The Office Building: From Concept to Investment Reality* (Chicago: Appraisal Institute, American Society of Real Estate Counselors, and Society of Industrial and Office Realtors, 1993).

Exhibit 3.3 **Illustration of Floor Area Ratios**

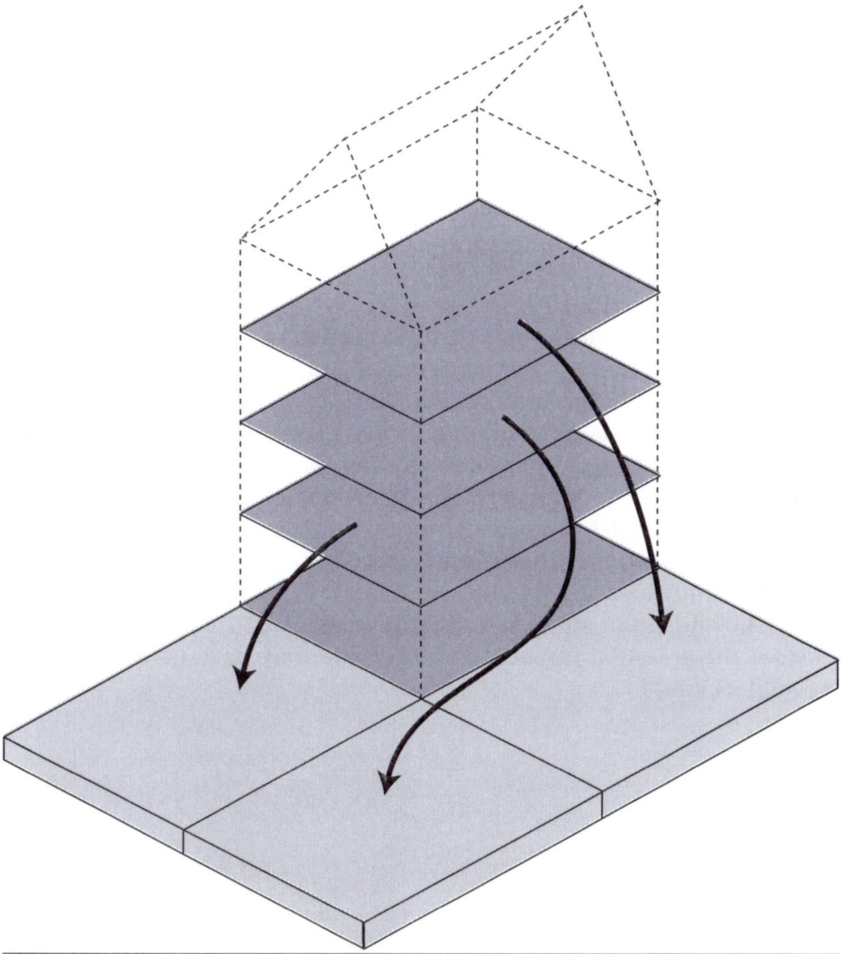

Source: CarFree.com Web site, *http://www.carfree.com/far.html*. Used with permission.

mon area maintenance. Encroachments may be disclosed on an ALTA survey by the client/owner or discovered as part of the on-site inspection. Encroachments can take many forms, including fences, building improvements, and vegetation (trees). The appraiser should determine the severity of the encroachment and the respective impact on value.

Location Analysis

The location of the subject site, with respect to important linkages, may impact the value of the property. Perhaps the first consideration in location analysis is a careful examination of adjacent and nearby uses. For instance, an office property that is adjacent to or near similar office properties and supporting uses (such as restaurants) would benefit from this location. On the other hand, an office property that is adjacent to or near heavy industrial properties, with no nearby supporting uses, would suffer from this location.

One very important location attribute is proximity to major transportation corridors, including freeways and toll roads. Easy access and close proximity to good transportation systems are well received by prospective tenants, resulting in a stronger rent roll.

Another important location attribute includes the demographics of the neighborhood. Office properties located in affluent areas typically command higher rents than similar properties in less affluent areas.

Environmental Issues

Office properties generally do not suffer from man-made environmental contaminants caused by negligent manufacturing processes, which are sometimes found in the industrial sector. However, office sites can be impacted by natural environmental issues such as wetlands, streams, or endangered species. Appraisers are not qualified to assess the environmental status of a property. However, the appraiser does have the responsibility to disclose any obvious environmental issues discovered during the inspection. If the appraiser suspects that environmental issues may limit or influence the development potential and/or future use of the site, he or she must actively investigate this issue and fully disclose the potential impact that this issue may have on the value of the subject site.

Chapter

4 Improvement Analysis

The primary objective of an improvement analysis is to carefully assess the physical characteristics of the building improvements to

1. Determine the highest and best use
2. Determine the relevant approaches to value
3. Acquire relevant data for future analysis in the three approaches to value

Preparing for the Inspection

The first step of the improvement analysis is to prepare for the inspection. This is accomplished by compiling all relevant data that may be readily available from the owner or client, such as plans and specifications, engineering studies, environmental reports, and the tenant rent roll. For the inspection, the appraiser typically brings a digital camera, relevant measuring instruments, and a clipboard. A checklist is typically used to ensure a thorough inspection and limit the number of follow-up visits. A properly performed inspection is absolutely essential for calculating a reliable estimate of value for the subject property; it also mitigates the probability of adverse legal action that may result from a poorly performed inspection.

Exterior Inspection

Building Placement on the Site

Generally, the appraiser begins the inspection with the exterior of the building, which follows nicely after the site inspection. Prior to approaching the building, the appraiser observes the building placement on the site and its orientation. Generally, office buildings facing the street provide the highest level of visibility, although exceptional views or other unique topographical or development issues may warrant an alternative orientation. If the benefit of an alternative orientation is not readily apparent, then functional obsolescence may exist. Exhibit 4.1 illustrates an office building site plan that shows the orientation of the building to the street and parking area.

Exhibit 4.1 **Office Building Site Plan**

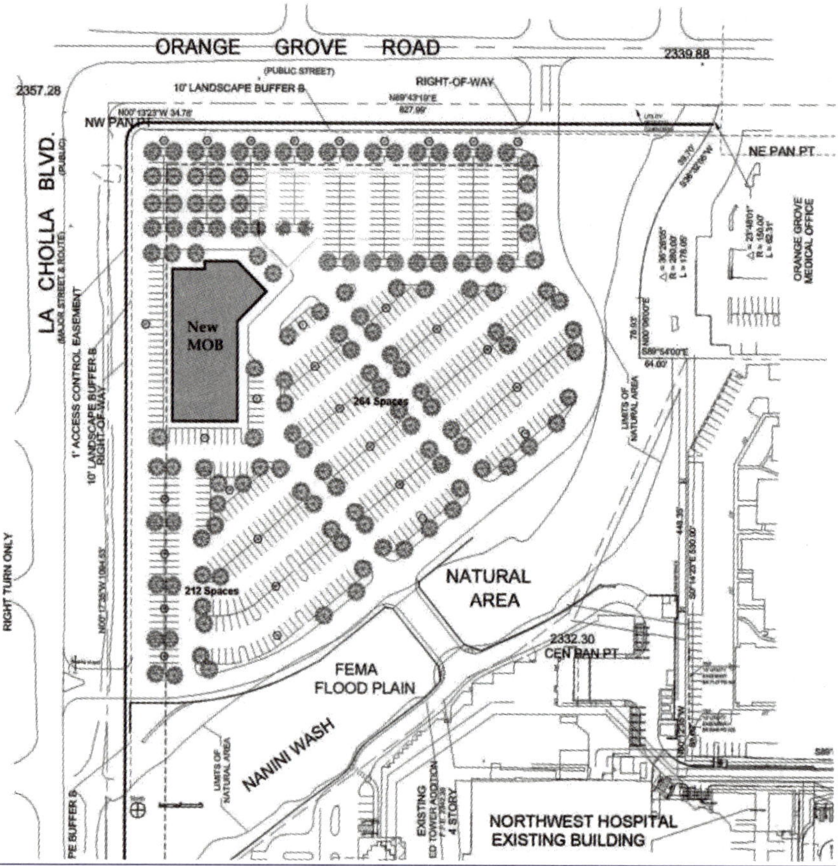

Source: Rendina Companies. © All rights reserved by Rendina Companies of America, LLC. Used with permission.

Exterior Photographs

As part of the exterior inspection, the appraiser typically takes photographs of the exterior, including views of the front and the rear of the building as well as the view of the building from the street. With the availability of today's digital photography equipment, the appraiser is encouraged to be liberal in taking photographs. The saying "a picture is worth a thousand words" definitely applies to real estate. Photographs in an appraisal report can provide more insight to readers than lengthy descriptions. In addition, the appraiser may need to refer back to the photographs to clarify some physical aspect of the property that may have been overlooked during the inspection. While taking photographs, the appraiser must note any obvious problems observed on or in the property, including significant items of deferred maintenance or physical deterioration.

Assessment of Quality and Condition

The exterior inspection allows the appraiser to verify the story height and type of building–i.e., mid-rise, bank branch, office with retail, etc. The exterior inspection also allows the appraiser to assess the quality and condition of the exterior walls, roof system, and windows. After construction, it is difficult for the appraiser to assess the quality and condition of the foundation and superstructure, but the appraiser can at least report the characteristics of these components derived from plans and specifications or conversations with the owner.

The quality and condition of the exterior walls can be directly observed. For the most part, exterior walls can be categorized as either *load bearing* or *self carrying*. Load-bearing walls support the floors and roof structure of the building, are generally found in low-rise structures, and exist primarily in older office buildings. Self-carrying walls are suspended from the superstructure and are generally found in modern office buildings.[1]

As with the exterior walls, the roof system is often observable to the appraiser. A roof system in poor condition will undoubtedly impact value due to the capital expense required to correct the problem. A leaking roof system can negatively impact the entire facility and will generally not be tolerated by the tenants; therefore, obvious signs of severe deterioration will require immediate attention and must be explicitly addressed in the valuation sections of the report.

Windows

From a valuation perspective, windows are perhaps one of the more important exterior characteristics of an office building due to their dual aesthetic and functional nature. The appraiser must be careful to not overlook this important physical characteristic in the inspection. For instance, the type of window–dual or single pane–can materially impact the energy efficiency of the building, thereby directly influencing the operating expenses. In addition, windows influence the general appeal of the building and are very important to the office occupants, especially the executives who make the leasing decisions. If the window placement enhances the views, ambience, lighting, and prestige of the office space, decision-making executives will pay a higher rent. On the other hand, if the window type, size, and placement limit these important characteristics, then the rent and occupancy levels may be negatively affected. Furthermore, investors have been known to purchase office properties with undesirable window features and realize significant increases in property value after making changes to this single component.

While inspecting the building exterior, the appraiser should also observe and take note of the general condition of all the exterior com-

1. For a more comprehensive examination of office building exterior walls, see John R. White, ed., *The Office Building: From Concept to Investment Reality* (Chicago: Appraisal Institute, American Society of Real Estate Counselors, and Society of Industrial and Office Realtors, 1993).

ponents of the property, paying particular attention to structural defects or obvious signs of physical deterioration that will require repair or replacement. In addition, the appraiser should investigate and determine the physical age and effective age of the property.

Interior Inspection

Interior Layout and Design

The functionality and flexibility of the interior layout and design is very important to the overall success of an office building. A rectangular design is considered the most efficient design because it allows elevators to be placed in the central building core.[2] Column spacing determines the size and location of the individual offices, as does the floor plate size. The floor plate is the horizontal layout of each floor in the office building. Column spacing and floor plate size can be influenced by local tastes and preferences–i.e., what the competition is doing.

Clear economies of scale in construction costs occur with larger buildings that have larger floor plates. However, these economies of scale are moderated with vertical construction. The taller the building, the more costly it is to build each additional floor. Still, regardless of building size, it is vital that the appraiser carefully examine the column spacing and floor plate size to determine the functionality of the interior layout, because this characteristic directly impacts the rents and occupancy of the building. Assessing the functionality of the interior layout is generally accomplished by investigating the characteristics of competing properties and interviewing office building occupants.

Interior Partitioning and Ceiling Height

Unlike the column spacing and floor plate size, the interior partitioning and ceiling height can generally be modified according to tenant preferences. In this regard, the appraiser observes and assesses the quality, condition, and functional layout of the interior build-out and makes an overall determination of its impact on property value. In some cases, the interior build-out may be of poor quality and condition, requiring significant renovation to make the property competitive. On the other hand, the interior quality and condition may be excellent, requiring little or no change.

Office Building Amenities and Services

Many office buildings, especially those located in a CBD, offer amenities such as restaurants, spas, athletic facilities, security guards, and child care. These amenities and services generally enhance the value of the property by positively impacting office rents. In addition, the building area occupied by specialty tenants may command premium rents. While the existing rent roll and history of these specialty suites often

---

2. Ibid.

Exhibit 4.2 Sample Floor Plate Design

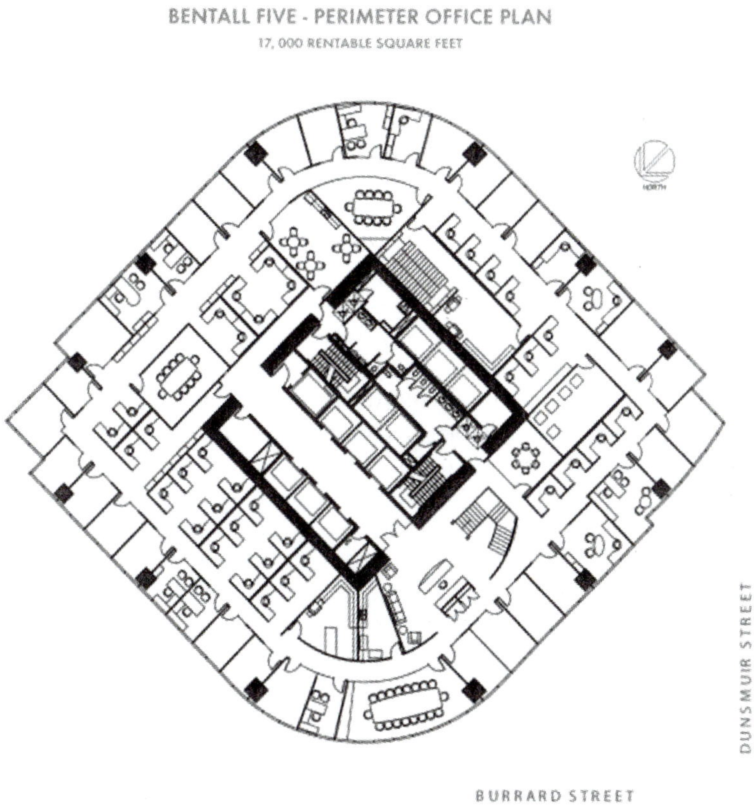

Source: Bentall Five Web site, *www.bentall5.com*. Owned by SITQ and developed/managed by Bentall LP. Used with permission.

provides the appraiser with an indication of the contributory value of the amenities, additional market research is generally required to properly estimate market rents and occupancy rates for these suites. The tenant improvements of ground-level retail or restaurant space can be significant and must be examined separately from the general office space.

Vertical Transportation

Escalators are frequently used to transport occupants from underground parking to the main lobby level, where elevators are located. The capacity, speed, and reliability of the vertical transportation are all very important to existing and prospective tenants and can significantly impact tenant satisfaction within the building. This is particularly true with elevators.[3] Therefore, the appraiser should carefully examine these

3. White, *The Office Building*.

characteristics during the inspection process and make a determination as to their functionality. Inadequate vertical transportation systems result in functional obsolescence. Inspections of transportation systems in competing office properties can assist with this assessment. In addition, brief questioning of building tenants about their satisfaction with the in-building transportation may provide insight.[4]

Electrical Capacity and Systems

Even though the appraiser may not have expertise in electrical systems, he or she should ascertain the general level of capacity and adequacy of the electrical system in the subject building. This can be done by examining the circuit box and interviewing the owner or client and tenants. If the building is fully occupied, interviews with the tenants may provide the most candid assessment of this item. If tenants complain of frequent electrical problems or concerns of adequacy, functional obsolescence must be addressed. A comparison of the electrical expense within competing buildings can also assist with this assessment. As firms continue to employ more technology, energy requirements will increase. On a positive note, however, light bulbs are becoming more energy efficient, and computer-managed mechanical and electrical systems are allowing for greater efficiency. Property owners are increasingly integrating sophisticated energy management computer systems to monitor electricity use and allocate it efficiently to minimize expense.

HVAC Systems

Existing and prospective tenants are very sensitive to the adequacy of heating, ventilation, and air-conditioning (HVAC) systems. In fact, rental and occupancy rates can be directly impacted by inadequate or problematic HVAC systems. In addition, the operating expenses may be influenced by the energy efficiency of the HVAC system. Therefore, the appraiser should carefully assess the adequacy, efficiency, and technological level of the HVAC system and compare these with competing properties. Characteristics most important to tenants include individual zones, flexibility of thermostat control, and the level of ventilation, including air cleaning systems. Inadequate ventilation and improper air cleaning systems can lead to *sick building syndrome*, which can negatively impact building occupants. A building is classified as a *sick building* when at least 20% of its occupants suffer persistent headaches and/or eye and mucus membrane irritation that are relieved when they leave the building. Additional symptoms include frequent colds, flu and respiratory infections, dizziness, fatigue, short-term memory loss, and

4. "An individual elevator that serves too many floors causes undue delays because it must make too many stops. Tall buildings thus may require zoned and even stacked elevators that can take up floor space and add to costs. Often the solution is to limit the size of the building rather than install a more expensive or more complicated elevator system" (White, *The Office Building*, 26).

hypersensitivity to pollutants.[5] The reputational effects of a sick building may materially impact rent and occupancy levels. The challenge in analyzing this form of obsolescence is estimating the cost to "cure" the problem and its offset increase in value.

Plumbing

In a general-purpose office building, plumbing is often limited to mechanical equipment and restrooms. Municipal construction codes typically control the extent and quality of the plumbing, making this a minor item in the building inspection. It is, however, important that the appraiser assess the adequacy and quality of the restrooms by interviewing tenants and conducting a physical inspection. Undersized or inadequate restroom facilities can result in tenant dissatisfaction with the building, potentially impacting rental and occupancy rates. On the other hand, oversized restrooms may create obsolescence via superadequacy. In any regard, the appraiser should inspect the restroom facilities and make a general assessment as to their adequacy.

Safety Systems

There is a high correlation between the class or quality of the building and the level of its safety systems. Higher-quality buildings tend to have more safety systems. These systems may include advanced smoke and fire alarms, sprinkler systems, emergency stairwells, firefighting equipment such as fire extinguishers and fire hoses, on-site security cameras, and related systems. Generally, the level of safety systems can be readily determined at the time of inspection.

Technological Capacity

There is an increasing demand for greater technological capability in office properties. The technological capability of an office building is generally determined by the level and adequacy of fiber optic lines, high-speed Internet wiring, cable television wiring, video conferencing capabilities, and computer-controlled heating and cooling systems. Buildings that have a high level of technological capacity (especially in the heating, cooling, and ventilation systems) are generally referred to as *smart buildings*.[6] As with safety systems, greater technological capacity generally leads to higher rents and values. In fact, older buildings with little or no technological capacity may suffer from severe functional obsolescence. An investigation of competing properties may provide the basis for determining the level of obsolescence, if any.

Americans with Disabilities Act

Appraisers need a general understanding of Americans with Disabilities Act (ADA) requirements, and these requirements should be explained in

---

5. Krisandra Guidry, "Sick Commercial Buildings: What Appraisers Need to Know," *The Appraisal Journal* (January 2002): 28.
6. White, *The Office Building*.

the appraisal report. *The Appraisal of Real Estate* makes the following statement regarding the Americans with Disabilities Act:

> An appraiser cannot assume that improvements comply with the requirements of the Americans with Disabilities Act (ADA) of 1990. Enforcement of the requirements can be triggered by a change in use or a title transfer. Owners of older properties may have to add ramps, elevators, or other special equipment to comply with ADA regulations, which can impact value greatly.
>
> Along with related legislation such as the Fair Housing Amendments Act of 1988 and the Uniform Federal Accessibility Standards, ADA extends protection under civil rights laws to people with disabilities. Among other provisions directed toward employment opportunities, the legislation guarantees access to places of public accommodation to persons with disabilities. Specifically, Title III of the act, which deals with "places of public accommodations" and "commercial facilities," is of particular importance to appraisers. Government publications regarding ADA are available online at *http://www.usdoj.gov/crt/ada/publicat.htm* and the ADA information line is 800-514-0301 (voice) or 800-514-0383 (TDD).
>
> A real estate appraiser is not required to become an expert in the field of ADA requirements, but the Competency Rule of the Uniform Standards of Professional Appraisal Practice requires appraisers to have the knowledge and experience necessary to complete a specific assignment competently or to disclose the lack of knowledge and experience to the client, take all steps necessary to complete the assignment competently, and in the report describe their lack of knowledge or experience and the steps taken to competently complete the assignment. Further guidance on ADA-related matters is provided in Guide Note 9: The Consideration of the Americans with Disabilities Act in the Appraisal Process, in the Guide Notes to the Standards of Professional Appraisal Practice of the Appraisal Institute.[7]

Older office buildings sometimes suffer from noncompliant handicapped parking spaces, inadequate restroom facilities, inaccessible entryways, and a lack of elevators. The potential cost of remedying these defects to place the property in compliance with the ADA may be significant and must be adequately addressed in the appraisal report.[8]

Environmental Issues

For the most part, office buildings do not suffer from detrimental environmental issues as much as industrial properties; however, it is important that the appraiser be aware of obvious potential problems. The most frequent environmental issue found in older office properties is asbestos. The appraiser should inquire as to the availability of environmental reports compiled for the property owner as well as interviewing the owner/client. If adverse environmental features are found in the building, the appraiser must take the necessary steps to address the impact on value. For example, if the property has asbestos, then the appraiser should determine if the asbestos is friable, encapsulated, or abated. Depending on the magnitude of the adverse environmental issue(s), the

7. *The Appraisal of Real Estate*, 13th ed. (Chicago: Appraisal Institute, 2008), 250.
8. For further discussion of ADA considerations in the valuation process, see Richard W. Hoyt and Robert J. Aalberts, "Appraisers and the Americans with Disabilities Act," *The Appraisal Journal* (July 1995): 298-309, and Robert J. Aalberts and Terrance M. Clauretie, "Commercial Real Estate and the Americans with Disabilities Act: Implications for Appraisers," *The Appraisal Journal* (July 1992): 53-58.

appraiser must fully report his or her findings and take the necessary steps to ensure that this issue is adequately addressed in the report.

Building Measurement

Building size provides the fundamental unit of comparison for office valuation, which is price per square foot and rent per square foot. Therefore, accurate and consistent measurement of the building area is essential to accurate valuation. The Building Owners and Managers Association (BOMA) International provides the industry standard for office building measurement.[9] However, many local markets do not adhere to BOMA's measurement criteria; therefore, it is incumbent upon the appraiser to determine the applicable criteria for the type of property and geographic area of the building being appraised and to clearly and consistently apply this criteria in the appraisal report.

The purpose of this section is to discuss and illustrate two of the more prominent measurement criteria so that appraisers can better understand and properly address this issue in their appraisal reports. Exhibit 4.3 compares building area definitions from the Appraisal Institute's *Dictionary of Real Estate Appraisal* with those outlined in BOMA's *Standard Method for Measuring Floor Area in Office Buildings.*

A careful study shows that BOMA's definitions differ from the Appraisal Institute's. Differences in building area calculations are also common in practice. For instance, the office building measurement criteria applied by local practitioners in Dallas may differ from the criteria applied by local practitioners in Manhattan. Periodically, the measurement criteria not only differs geographically but also by property type and size (i.e., measurements of larger buildings frequently follow the BOMA criteria while measurements of smaller buildings frequently follow a simpler criteria). Because of these inconsistencies, it is especially important that the appraiser clearly identify and define the measurement criteria used for the subject property and then consistently apply the same criteria to comparable properties.

BOMA Measurement Criteria

BOMA tends to represent larger office properties, and BOMA building measurement standards are usually employed in larger properties located in a large metropolitan area CBD. When using BOMA building measurement criteria, the appraiser first calculates the relevant building area measures defined as follows:

> ***Gross building area*** shall mean the total constructed area of a building. It is generally not used for leasing purposes.

9. In 1915, BOMA International established standard methods for measuring floor areas in office buildings. The purpose of these standards was "to permit clear communication and computation on a clear and understandable basis," according to BOMA International's 1996 document, *Standard Method for Measuring Floor Area in Office Buildings*.

Exhibit 4.3	Comparison of Building Measurement Definitions
Appraisal Institute Definition	**BOMA Definition**
Gross Building Area The total floor area of a building, including below-grade space but excluding unenclosed areas, measured from the exterior of the walls. Gross building area for office buildings is computed by measuring to the outside finished surface of permanent outer building walls without any deductions. All enclosed floors of the building including basements, mechanical equipment floors, penthouses, and the like are included in the measurement. Parking spaces and parking garages are excluded.	Gross building area shall mean the total constructed area of a building. It is generally not used for leasing purposes. This area is computed by measuring to the outside finished surface of permanent outer building walls, without any deductions. All enclosed floors of the building, including basements, garages, mechanical equipment floors, penthouses, and the like, are calculated.
Rentable Area The amount of space on which the rent is based; calculated according to local practice.	Rentable area shall mean the usable area of an office area or store area with its associated share of floor common areas and building common areas. Rentable area is determined by multiplying the usable area of an office area or store area by the *R/U* ratio. The total of all rentable areas equals the building rentable area for the building.
Usable Area The area available for assignment or rental to an occupant, including every type of usable space; measured from the inside finish of outer walls to the office side of corridors or permanent partitions and from the centerline of adjacent spaces; includes subdivided occupant space, but no deductions are made for columns and projections. There are two variations of net area: single occupant net assignable area and store net assignable area.	Usable area shall mean the measured area of an office area, store area, or building common area on a floor. The total of all the usable areas for a floor shall equal floor usable area of that same floor. Floor usable area shall be computed by measuring the area enclosed between the finished surface of the office area side of corridors and the dominant portion and/or major vertical penetrations. Building common areas are considered to be part of floor usable area. No deduction shall be made for columns and projections necessary to the building. Where alcoves, recessed entrances, or similar deviation from the corridor line are present, floor usable area shall be computed as if the deviation were not present.

Source: *The Dictionary of Real Estate Appraisal*, 4th ed. (Chicago: Appraisal Institute, 2002), and BOMA International, *Standard Method for Measuring Floor Area in Office Buildings*, 1996. (BOMA document available for purchase through BOMA International's Web site at *www.boma.org*.)

Gross measured area shall mean the total area of a building enclosed by the *dominant portion*, excluding parking areas and loading docks (or portions of the same) outside the building line. It is generally not used for leasing purposes and is calculated on a floor-by-floor basis.

Dominant portion shall mean the portion of the inside *finished surface* of the permanent outer building wall, which is 50% or more of the vertical floor-to-ceiling dimension, at the given point being measured as one moves horizontally along the wall. *Dominant portion* itself is a vertical measurement between *finished surfaces* (or a series of vertical measurements), with the number of measurements needed based upon the conditions found along the wall. If, for instance, a window system is 4'6" (1.372 meters) high and the floor to ceiling dimension is 9'0" (2.743 meters), the *dominant portion* is the inside surface of the glass for the full width of the window system. If, however, the window system is 4'5" (1.346 meters), the *dominant portion* is the inside surface of the wall. In designs of alternating window systems and wall sections, the *dominant portion* will move in and out as often as conditions dictate. If no *finished surface* of the permanent outer building wall is 50% or more of the vertical floor-to-ceiling dimension, or if the permanent outer building wall is not vertical, the *dominant portion* shall be the inside finished surface of the wall where it intersects the finished floor. In the case of *store area* with street level frontage, the *dominant portion* shall be the building line.

Finished surface shall mean a wall, ceiling or floor surface, including glass, as prepared for tenant use, excluding the thickness of any special surfacing materials such as paneling, furring strips, and/or carpet.[10]

Exhibit 4.4 illustrates the dominant portion of exterior walls.

Exhibit 4.4 **Dominant Portion of Exterior Walls**

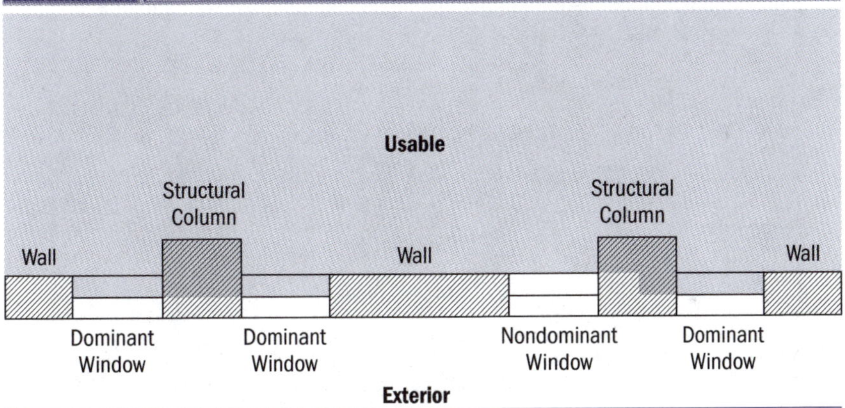

Source: LaserTech Floor Plans. Used with permission. (LaserTech is the official interpreter of the BOMA measurement standards, appointed in 2004, and as such endorses and supports the standard implementation of BOMA standards.)

After calculating the gross measured area of the office building, the appraiser then deducts major vertical penetrations on each floor to calculate the floor rentable area (FRA). Exhibits 4.5 and 4.6 provide lease plans for a two-story office building. The *major vertical penetrations* are identified with dark grey shading. BOMA uses the following definitions:

Floor rentable area shall mean the result of subtracting from the *gross measured area* of a floor the ***major vertical penetrations*** on that same floor. It is generally fixed for the life of the building and is rarely affected by changes in corridor size or configuration.

Major vertical penetrations shall mean stairs, elevator shafts, flues, pipe shafts, vertical ducts and the like, and their enclosing walls. Atria, lightwells, and similar

10. BOMA International, *Standard Method for Measuring Floor Area in Office Buildings*, 1996.

penetrations above the finished floor are included in this definition. Not included, however, are vertical penetrations built for the private use of a tenant occupying *office areas* on more than one floor. Structural columns, openings for vertical electric cable or telephone distribution, and openings for plumbing lines are not considered to be major vertical penetrations.[11]

After calculating the FRA, the appraiser then calculates the *floor usable area* (FUA), which is the usable area on each floor. FUA is defined as follows:

> ***Usable area*** shall mean the measured area of an ***office area***, ***store area***, or ***building common area*** on a floor. The total of all the ***usable areas*** for a floor shall equal the ***floor usable area*** of that same floor.

Exhibit 4.5 Main Floor Lease Plan

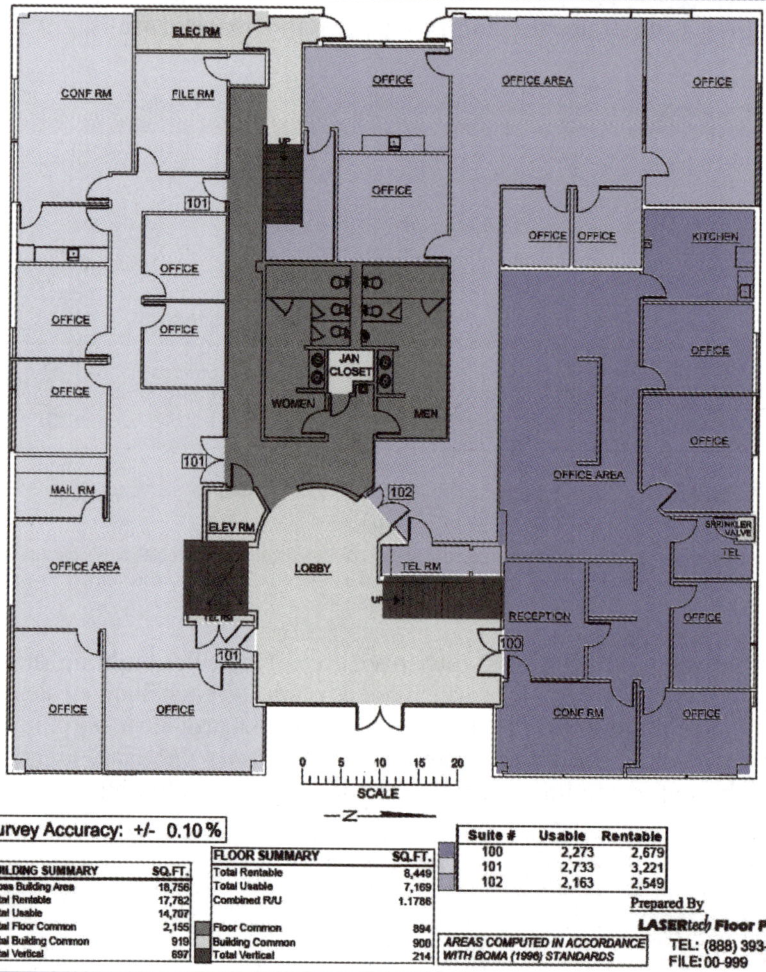

Survey Accuracy: +/- 0.10 %

BUILDING SUMMARY	SQ.FT.
Gross Building Area	18,756
Total Rentable	17,782
Total Usable	14,707
Total Floor Common	2,155
Total Building Common	919
Total Vertical	697

FLOOR SUMMARY	SQ.FT.
Total Rentable	8,449
Total Usable	7,169
Combined R/U	1.1786
Floor Common	894
Building Common	900
Total Vertical	214

Suite #	Usable	Rentable
100	2,273	2,679
101	2,733	3,221
102	2,163	2,549

AREAS COMPUTED IN ACCORDANCE WITH BOMA (1996) STANDARDS

Prepared By
LASERtech Floor Plans
TEL: (888) 393-6655
FILE: 00-999

Source: LaserTech Floor Plans. Used with permission.

11. Ibid.

Exhibit 4.6 **Second Floor Lease Plan**

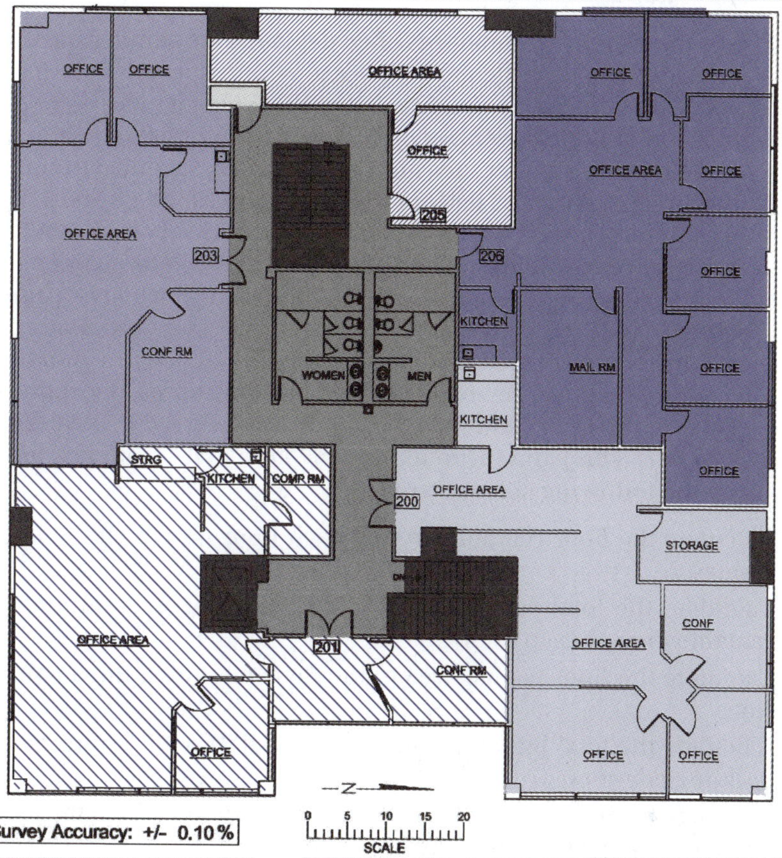

Survey Accuracy: +/- 0.10 %

FLOOR SUMMARY	SQ.FT.
Total Rentable	9,333
Total Usable	7,539
Combined R/U	1.2380
Floor Common	1,261
Building Common	20
Total Vertical	484

Suite #	Usable	Rentable
200	1,608	1,990
201	1,759	2,178
203	1,506	1,865
205	649	803
206	2,017	2,497

AREAS COMPUTED IN ACCORDANCE WITH BOMA (1996) STANDARDS

Prepared By
LASERtech Floor Plans
TEL: (888) 393-6655
FILE: 00-999

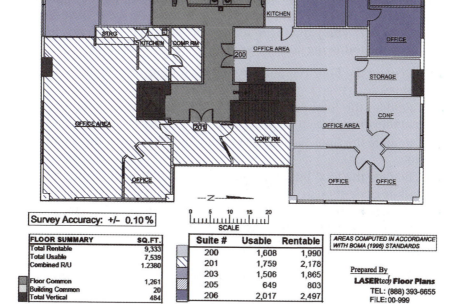

Source: LaserTech Floor Plans. Used with permission.

Office area shall mean the area where a tenant normally houses personnel and/or furniture, for which a measurement is to be computed.

Store area shall mean the area of an office building suitable for retail occupancy. *Store areas* are included in *floor rentable area* and *rentable area*.

Building common area shall mean the areas of the building that provide services to building tenants but which are not included in the *office area* or *store area* of any specific tenant. These areas may include, but shall not be limited to, main and auxiliary lobbies, atrium spaces at the level of the finished floor, concierge areas or security desks, conference rooms, lounges or vending areas, food service facilities, health or fitness centers, daycare facilities, locker or shower facilities, mail rooms, fire control rooms, fully enclosed courtyards outside the exterior walls, and building core and service areas such as fully enclosed mechanical or equipment rooms. Specifically excluded from *building common area* are *floor common area*, parking space, portions of loading docks outside the building line, and major vertical penetrations.[12]

BOMA measurement standards often deviate from simpler measurement criteria. This is particularly the case with respect to floor usable area. Notice that the BOMA definition of usable area includes *office area*, *store area*, and *building common area*. *Building common area* is generally not included in simpler measurement standards applied to smaller buildings in secondary and tertiary markets. In Exhibits 4.5 and 4.6, the building common area is white–i.e., not shaded. It is very important that the appraiser clearly differentiate between *building common area* and *floor common area*. *Floor common area* is common area that is "primarily for the use of tenants on that floor," while *building common area* is generally the common area that is used by all tenants in the building.

After estimating the previously defined building areas, the appraiser can calculate the *floor load factor* (sometimes referred to as the *floor combined R/U ratio*) and the total rentable area (TRA) for each tenant by using the following six-step process:

1. Calculate the floor rentable area of each floor on which the tenant resides.
2. Calculate the total rentable area of the building by summing the rentable area of each floor.
3. Calculate the floor usable area of the floor on which the tenant resides.
4. Calculate the total building common area (TBCA) by summing the building common area of each floor.
5. Calculate the floor load factor (FLF) for the floor on which the tenant resides by using the following equation:

$$FLF = \frac{FRA}{FUA - \left(\frac{FRA}{TRA}\right)(TBCA)}$$

Where

FLF = floor load factor (See the appendix at the end of this chapter for derivation of the FLF equation.)

FRA = floor rentable area

FUA = floor usable area

TRA = total rentable area

$TBCA$ = total building common area

6. Apply the FLF to the office or store usable area of an individual tenant to calculate the total rentable area for the tenant on that floor.

12. Ibid.

For example, assume the following area calculations:

$$FRA = 8{,}963$$
$$FUA = 8{,}063$$
$$TRA = 17{,}782$$
$$TBCA = 919$$

Then,

$$FLF = \frac{8{,}963}{8{,}063 - \left(\frac{8{,}963}{17{,}782}\right)(919)} = 1.1786$$

Next, assume that a tenant on the floor has 2,273 square feet of usable area. The rentable area is calculated by multiplying the usable area by the floor load factor (2,273 sq. ft. × 1.1786 = 2,679 sq. ft.).

Alternative Measurement Criteria

Due to the complexity and precision required to reliably prepare calculations according to the BOMA building measurement criteria, property owners and market participants associated with smaller properties in secondary and tertiary markets frequently employ a much simpler building measurement criteria as follows:

1. Calculate the gross measured area as previously defined.
2. Calculate the rentable area by deducting major vertical penetrations.
3. Calculate the usable area as the tenants' area under lock and key.[13]
4. Calculate the common area as the difference between rentable and usable area.
5. Calculate the building load factor by dividing the rentable area by the usable area.
6. Calculate each tenant's rentable area by multiplying the tenant's usable area by the building load factor.

To illustrate this particular alternative measurement technique, consider the floor plans for a small two-story office building shown in Exhibits 4.7 and 4.8. The building areas (see Exhibit 4.9) have been calculated using the alternative measurement technique.

Note that even though a simpler method for calculating building area may be enticing, the appraiser should adhere to BOMA standards if it is specified as such in the lease or leases. LaserTech, the official interpreter of the BOMA measurement standards, does not endorse or support non-standard building measurement methods.

13. John A. Simpson, *Property Inspection: An Appraiser's Guide* (Chicago: Appraisal Institute, 1997).

Exhibit 4.7 Main Floor Plan

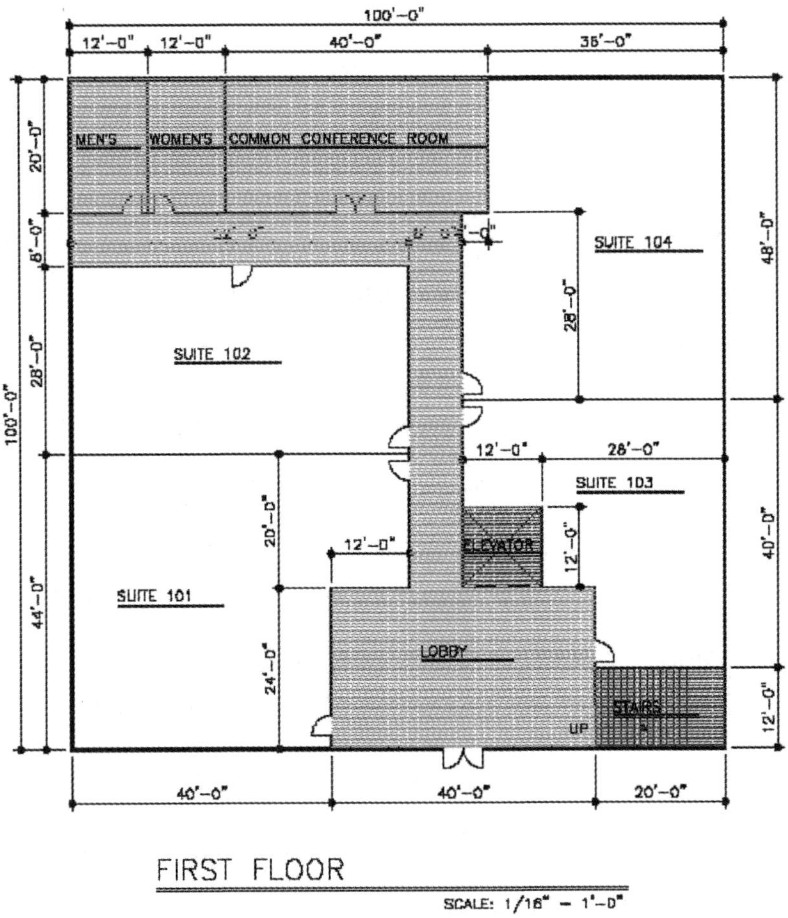

Exhibit 4.8 **Second Floor Plan**

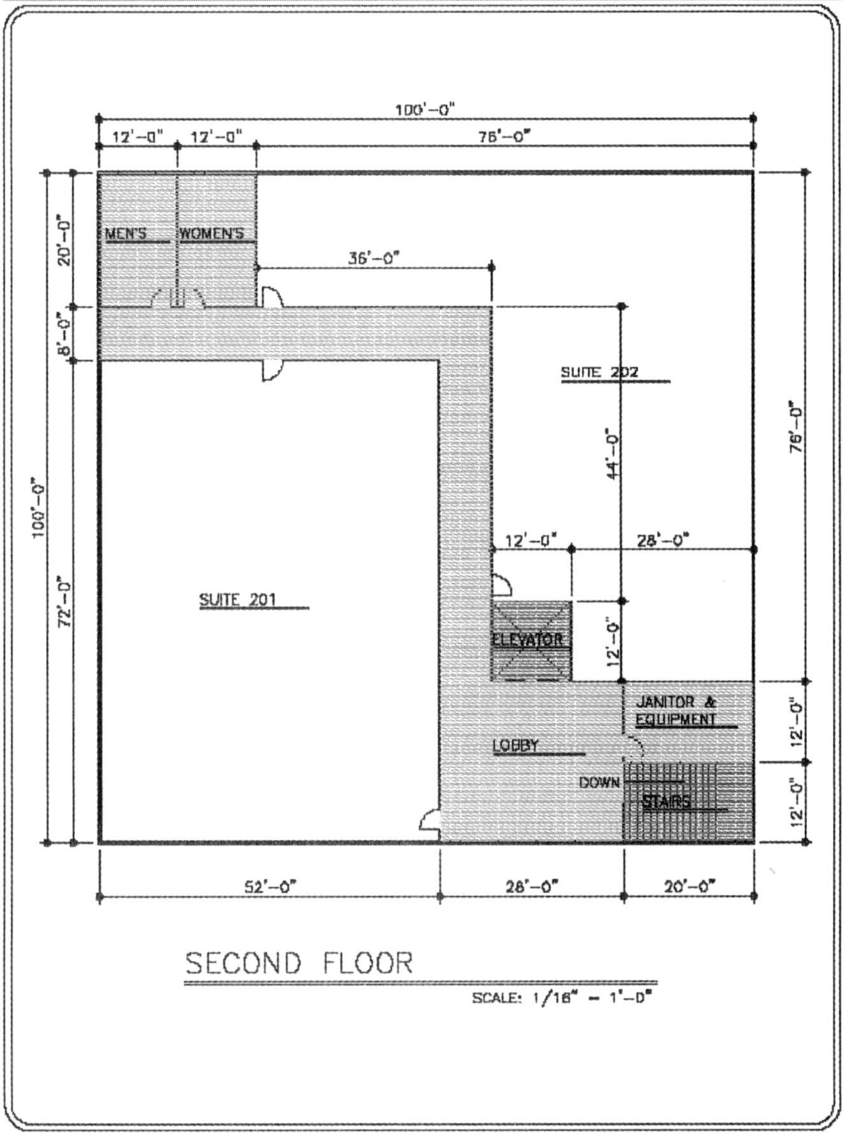

Exhibit 4.9 Building Area Calculations	
First Floor	**Square Feet**
Gross measured area	10,000
Rentable	9,616
Usable	6,512
Individual areas	
Suite 101	2,000
Suite 102	1,456
Suite 103	1,216
Suite 104	1,840
Restrooms	480
Conference room	800
Lobby	960
Hallways	864
Elevator	144
Stairs	240
Second Floor	
Gross measured area	10,000
Rentable	9,616
Usable	7,360
Individual areas	
Suite 201	3,744
Suite 202	3,616
Restrooms	480
Lobby	672
Janitorial/equipment room	240
Hallways	864
Elevator	144
Stairs	240
Total Building Areas	
Gross measured area	20,000
Rentable	19,232
Usable	13,872
Load factor	1.3864
Efficiency ratio	0.9616

Miscellaneous Considerations

When using plans to calculate the building area for an existing building, it is important to spot-check the plans with actual on-site measurements to verify their reliability. In addition, it is very important that the appraiser disclose in the report the extent that he or she relied upon third-party information in the building measurement section. It is absolutely essential that the appraiser also use the same measurement criteria for the comparables.

The appraiser can analyze the functionality and competitive position of the property by comparing the subject's load factor with the comparables. Higher load factors infer more common area, which may or may not be desired by the tenants. The efficiency ratio, calculated by dividing the rentable area by the gross building area, also provides an indication of the competitive position of the property. Properties with very high efficiency ratios may suffer from inadequate transportation systems–i.e., inadequate elevators, escalators, or stairs.[14] Very low efficiency ratios, however, may suggest obsolescence via superadequacy, resulting in excessive maintenance costs, such as too many elevators for which tenants will not pay a premium.

Building Classification

After the appraiser has performed a thorough inspection of the property, he or she is now ready to determine the proper classification of the building. Office building classifications are typically categorized as *Class A*, *Class B*, or *Class C*. Building classifications provide a basis for comparison as well as insight into the building's competitive ability to attract similar tenants and investors. A building's class is influenced by local tradition and can vary across geographic areas, although standard determinants often include location, rent level, exterior and interior finishes, the technological level of systems, and market perception. Exhibit 4.10 summarizes the typical determinants of office building classification.

It is important to observe that market participants in each geographic area ultimately determine the classification criteria. As a result, it is essential that the appraiser investigate the local criteria and use this information in the appraisal process to assist with the data research and acquisition. The appraiser must clearly explain the criteria in the appraisal

Exhibit 4.10 Office Building Classifications

Class A	Class B	Class C
· Most prestigious buildings	· Wide range of users	· Older/tired buildings
· Premier users	· Average rents	· Below-average rents
· Above-average rents	· Average quality finishes	· Below-average finishes
· High-quality finishes	· Adequate/average systems	· Semi-functional space
· State-of-the-art systems		· Minimum systems
· Exceptional location		

14. "The efficiency ratio should be 85% or greater. If the subject has a lower efficiency ratio than comparable buildings of the same class, an adjustment for functional obsolescence may be required" (Simpson, *Property Inspection*).

report because lenders, brokers, attorneys, and other possible readers of the report rely on the appraiser for an assessment of this item.

Building Condition

The building condition is determined subjectively during the inspection. Determinants typically include obvious signs of wear and tear such as peeling paint, a leaking roof, cracked concrete, an outdated carpet, etc. After performing the inspection and considering the competitive position of the subject property, the appraiser makes an overall determination of building condition by describing it as excellent, good, average, fair, or poor. The appraiser carefully describes his or her findings in the appraisal report and the reasoning for his or her conclusion. The appraiser also uses this information in the collection of market data and in the other analysis sections of the appraisal.

Building Utility and Marketability

Firms acquire or lease office space to facilitate their business objectives. A building's characteristics can influence the firm's image as well as affect employee productivity. The exterior facade and interior finish can impact the firm's image. The floor plate design or interior configuration, communications systems, parking, and elevator capacity are all components that may influence utility and marketability. Buildings with greater utility generally command higher rents, which impact the marketability and value of the property. Therefore, the appraiser must carefully consider these issues and appropriately address them in valuation sections of the appraisal.

Green Buildings

Appraisers are increasingly encountering valuation questions that relate to "green" office properties. However, many appraisers are not adequately informed about this contemporary topic. Therefore, the objective of this section is to provide a brief overview with a specific emphasis on valuation issues.

Green Building Defined

What is building "green"? The essence of building green is constructing new buildings or remodeling existing buildings so that they are environmentally friendly and longer lasting. Green building development–also referred to as *whole*, *sustainable*, *environmental*, or *natural buildings*, *development*, or *design*–uses "design and construction practices that meet specified standards, resolving much of the negative impact of buildings on their occupants and on the environment."[15] The 1987 report of

15. Michael Jeppesen, "What Makes a Green Building Green?" *Green Earth Development* (August 2007), *http://www.greenearthdev.com/ai/What_makes_a_building_Green.pdf.*

the World Commission on Environment and Development provides a similar definition: "Sustainable development is development that meets the needs of the present without compromising the ability of future generations to meet their own needs."[16] *Building Design and Construction* magazine offers a more detailed definition, explaining that building green increases the efficiency with which buildings and their sites use energy, water, and materials and reduces building impact on human health and the environment through better siting, design, construction, operation, maintenance, and removal (the complete building life cycle) as defined by the Office of Federal Environmental Executives.[17]

Why build green? One of the major reasons that companies choose to build green is escalating energy costs. According to Jim Broughton in his article *Cost, Savings, and Value: Part 1*, the increase in energy prices has made conserving energy and mitigating the risk of future price increases more attractive for many companies. Since 2001, natural gas, electricity, and OPEC oil have increased 117%, 18%, and 196% respectively, motivating companies to find ways to keep their energy costs low. Because green buildings are specifically constructed to be more energy efficient, many companies opt to build green to reduce their energy expenses.[18]

A second major reason why companies choose to build green is a desire to be more environmentally responsible. The Environmental Protection Agency offers the following statistics:

- Buildings account for 39.4% of total U.S. energy consumption. Commercial buildings account for 45.4% of that total.
- Buildings account for 67.9% of total U.S. electricity consumption, 48.8% of which is attributed to commercial buildings.
- Buildings account for 12.2% of the total water consumed in the United States per day. Commercial buildings account for 25.6%.
- The percentage of total carbon dioxide emissions attributed to buildings in the United States is 38.1%. Commercial buildings contribute 17.5% to that total.[19]

Because commercial buildings are accountable for such a large portion of energy consumption and pollution in the United States, many companies feel that building green is the environmentally responsible thing to do. Some companies build green purely for the environmental benefits, while others hope to boost their company's image by being socially responsible.[20]

---

16. Scott Muldavin, "A Strategic Response to Sustainable Property Investing," *The Pension Real Estate Association* (Summer 2007): 37-40.
17. "A Brief History of Green Building," *Building Design and Construction* (November 2003): 4-7.
18. Jim Johnson, "It's Green, and It's Building," *Waste News* (April 30, 2007); Jim Broughton, "Costs, Savings, and Value: Part One," *Environmental Design and Construction* (November 2006): 110-116.
19. "Buildings and the Environment: A Statistical Summary." U.S. Environmental Protection Agency, 2004. Available online at *http://www.epa.gov/greenbuilding/pubs/gbstats.pdf*.
20. Marianne Wilson, "Taking the LEED," *Chain Store Age* (March 2005): 45-52.

The Cost of Building Green

One of the largest issues regarding building green is the cost required to incorporate green building standards. In their article *What Does Green Really Cost?*, Morris and Langdon comment that "people who are green-adverse are happy to relate anecdotes of premiums in excess of 30% to make their buildings green... [but] it is clear from the substantial weight of evidence in the marketplace that reasonable levels of sustainable design can be incorporated into most building types at little or no additional cost."[21] Suttell supports this claim, explaining that "it costs anywhere from nothing more to a nominal amount more to build green over the budget for a traditionally designed building."[22]

Jim Broughton, in his article *Costs, Savings, and Value*, gives average cost premiums for each of the four levels of designated Leadership in Energy and Environmental Design (LEED) certification, clearly demonstrating that building green does not necessarily require a lot of money. According to the article, which is based on a study of 33 LEED projects,

- Certified (bronze) buildings have an average cost premium of 0.66%.
- The average cost premium for silver buildings is 2.11%.
- Gold buildings have an average cost premium of 1.82%.
- The average cost premium for platinum buildings is 6.50%.

The average premium for the 33 LEED buildings is 1.84%, which is considerably lower than the cost premium many green building cynics site. According to Jim Johnson, "If you spend more than 3% [extra], you don't know what you're doing."[23]

The key to keeping green building costs low, however, is to incorporate green building design from the beginning and as a whole, rather than piecemeal. When green building designs are not established up front, or if the decision to build green is made once construction has begun, construction costs are more likely to increase.[24]

The Benefits of Building Green

Reportedly, the benefits of incorporating green features into buildings outweigh the costs that may be required and are a major reason why many companies are attracted to building green. Potential benefits that convince businesses to make the decision to go green include (but are not limited to) the following:

---

21. Peter Morris and Davis Langdon, "What Does Green Really Cost?" *PREA Quarterly* (Summer 2007): 55-60.
22. Robin Suttell, "The True Costs of Building Green," *Buildings* (April 2006): 46-48.
23. Jim Broughton, "Costs, Savings, and Value: Part Two," *Environmental Design and Construction* (December 2006): 40-42; Jim Johnson, "Building Green Doesn't Mean Spending Green," *Waste News* (April 30, 2007).
24. Suttell, "The True Costs of Building Green," 47; Broughton, "Costs, Savings, and Value: Part Two," 41.

- Minimized effects on the environment
- Higher net operating incomes and appraised value as well as better financial leverage
- Higher lease rates and occupancy rates
- Properties lease more quickly
- The ability to reallocate financial resources saved as a result of green design
- Reduced operating expenses for utilities, repairs, and maintenance
- Increased worker productivity, decreased absenteeism, and improved quality of work performed by employees by as much as 10 to 15% because of improved air quality, comfort, daylighting, and energy efficiency
- The ability to recruit and retain top employees
- Increased employee morale and loyalty and reduced employee turnover
- For retail stores, higher sales specifically attributed to daylighting
- Property tax incentives for reducing city government infrastructure costs and business income tax deductions for qualifying green
- Lower insurance costs due to decreased health-related liabilities[25]

Companies that have opted to pursue green building, such as Starbucks, Giant Eagle, Target, Home Depot, and Aveda, confirm that the financial and environmental benefits of building green far outweigh the costs.

Valuation Issues

The existing literature tends to depict a positive outlook for green buildings; however, the valuation impact is still very uncertain and must be examined on a case-by-case basis. The contemporary discussion in the popular press indicates that this issue is becoming more important to many office users such as government agencies and large national and multinational firms. These trends could have a direct impact on the absorption and rental rates of green office buildings, which may have a ripple effect on the entire office market. In the valuation process, the appraiser must carefully consider the potential incremental construction costs, operating efficiencies, revenue increases, and occupancy gains from green office buildings and then carefully articulate the findings and valuation impact in the appraisal report.

25. Aidan Stretch, "Design for the Environment and the Bottom Line," *Assessment Journal*, vol. 4, no. 1 (January/February 1997): 61; Jim Broughton, "Costs, Savings, and Value: Part Three," *Environmental Design and Construction* (January 2007): 22-24; Broughton, "Costs, Savings, and Value: Part One," 110; Broughton, "Costs, Savings, and Value: Part Two," 40-42.

Appendix.
Derivation of Floor Load Factor

Note the following equalities:

$$\frac{\frac{FRA}{TRA}(TBCA)}{FUA}=\frac{TFRA-OA\left(\frac{FRA}{FUA}\right)}{TFRA} \qquad (1)$$

Then

$$\frac{\frac{FRA}{TRA}(TBCA)}{FUA}=1-\frac{OA\left(\frac{FRA}{FUA}\right)}{TFRA} \qquad (2)$$

Then

$$\frac{OA\left(\frac{FRA}{FUA}\right)}{TFRA}=1-\frac{\frac{FRA}{TRA}(TBCA)}{FUA} \qquad (3)$$

Then

$$TFRA=\frac{OA\left(\frac{FRA}{FUA}\right)}{1-\frac{\frac{FRA}{TRA}(TBCA)}{FUA}} \qquad (4)$$

Also note the following:

$$OA(FLF)=TFRA \qquad (5)$$

Then

$$FLF=\frac{TFRA}{OA} \qquad (6)$$

Then substitute equation (4) for TFRA in equation (6).

$$FLF=\frac{\dfrac{OA\left(\frac{FRA}{FUA}\right)}{1-\frac{\frac{FRA}{TRA}(TBCA)}{FUA}}}{OA} \qquad (7)$$

This can be simplified to

$$FLF=\frac{\left(\frac{FRA}{FUA}\right)}{1-\frac{\left(\frac{FRA}{TRA}\right)(TBCA)}{FUA}} \qquad (8)$$

$$FLF = \frac{FRA}{FUA\left[1 - \left(\frac{\left(\frac{FRA}{TRA}\right)(TBCA)}{FNA}\right)\right]} \tag{9}$$

$$FLF = \frac{FRA}{FUA - \left(\frac{FRA}{TRA}\right)(TBCA)} \tag{10}$$

Where

FRA = floor rentable area

TRA = total rentable area (sum of FRA on each floor)

TBCA = total building common area (sum of building common area on each floor)

FUA = floor usable area

TFRA = total floor rentable area

OA = office area

FLF = floor load factor

A tenant's rentable area is calculated by multiplying its usable office area or store area by the FLF.

Note: The FLF is synonymous with the BOMA combined *R*/*U* ratio.

Chapter 5

The Income Capitalization Approach

This chapter on the income capitalization approach is of great importance because market participants place considerable weight on this approach in the appraisal of office properties, which are frequently bought and sold based on their income-producing potential. This chapter consists of the following sections:

- Section 1 outlines the theoretical premise and methodology of the income capitalization approach.
- Section 2 investigates various lease types and important terms frequently encountered when appraising office properties.
- Section 3 introduces a case study (on a hypothetical office property) that provides a practical application of the material.
- Section 4 illustrates techniques for estimating rents and vacancies.
- Section 5 shows the proper analysis of operating expenses, leasing commissions, and capital costs.
- Section 6 summarizes the data and analysis generated in the previous sections.
- Section 7 outlines the theory and application of both the direct capitalization and yield capitalization techniques.
- Section 8 provides the reconciliation of the income capitalization approach to value.
- Section 9 shows alternative valuation scenarios to the base case.

Section 1. Theoretical Premise and Methodology of Income Capitalization

The income capitalization approach to value is based on the premise that income-producing properties are typically purchased as an investment; therefore, anticipated net revenue and yield are critical elements that affect the property's value. The formal definition of the *income capitalization approach* is

> A set of procedures through which an appraiser derives a value indication for an income-producing property by converting its anticipated benefits (cash flows and reversion) into property value. This conversion can be accomplished in two ways. One year's income expectancy can be capitalized at a market-derived capitalization rate or at a capitalization rate that reflects a specified income pattern, return on investment, and change in the value of the investment. Alternatively, the annual cash flows for the holding period and the reversion can be discounted at a specified yield rate.[1]

Property Interest Appraised

Determining the proper methodology to use in the income capitalization approach requires the appraiser to carefully identify the property interest being appraised. When a property is occupied with tenants that have valid leases, the client typically requests that the appraiser estimate the market value of the *leased fee interest*, which is an ownership interest held by a landlord with the rights of use and occupancy conveyed by lease to others. The rights of the lessor (the leased fee owner) and lessee are specified by contract terms within the lease.

This leased fee interest is the estate that is typically conveyed and purchased by sellers and buyers of office properties, and it is of greatest importance to prospective lenders. When underwriting a loan, the lender looks to the cash flows (leases) obtained from the tenants to meet the mortgage payments. Therefore, the lender is particularly concerned with the value of the property with the leases in place.

If a property is proposed, unoccupied (vacant), or owner occupied, the client will typically ask the appraiser to value the fee simple interest in the property. The *fee simple interest* or *fee simple estate* is absolute ownership unencumbered by any other interest or estate, subject only to the limitations imposed by the governmental powers of taxation, eminent domain, police power, and escheat.

When valuing the leased fee interest, the appraiser analyzes and considers the existing leases and related revenue, the occupancy, and the current and historical operating expenses. In other words, the appraiser focuses on the actual performance of the subject property and then investigates market rents, occupancies, and operating expenses to benchmark the actual property performance with competing properties. However, when valuing the fee simple interest, the appraiser considers and analyzes only market rents, occupancies, and operating expenses. Since the valuation process is different depending on the interest appraised, it is imperative that the appraiser clearly communicate with the client to ensure that the interest appraised meets the client's objectives. Once the appraiser has determined the proper interest to appraise, he or she can begin to collect and analyze the relevant data and value the property.

---

1. Unless otherwise noted, all definitions of terms in this chapter are taken from *The Dictionary of Real Estate Appraisal*, 4th ed. (Chicago: Appraisal Institute, 2002).

The valuation discussion in this chapter–as well as the discussions in Chapters 6 and 7 that deal with the sales comparison and cost approaches–all begin with detailed examinations of the valuation of the leased fee interest, assuming that the property status is "as is" and the property occupancy is stabilized. This is the base valuation scenario. Some alternative valuation scenarios will also be discussed.

Annual Operating Statement

There are three important financial statements in corporate finance.

- The balance sheet
- The income statement
- The statement of cash flows

Corporate managers and investors analyze these statements to gain insight into the financial health of the firm and assess its value. Similarly, in real estate there are two primary financial statements.

- The annual operating statement
- The reversion statement

Like corporate financial statements, the annual operating and reversion statements provide market participants with insights into the financial health of the property and the basis for its valuation. In practice, the annual operating statement generally takes one of two forms–conventional or contemporary.

A) Conventional Operating Statement

The following is a conventional operating statement:

Annual Operating Statement

	Potential gross income (*PGI*)
–	Vacancy and collection loss (V&CL)
+	Other income (*OI*)
	Effective gross income (*EGI*)
–	Operating expenses (*OE*)
–	Replacement allowance/reserves (*RES*)
	Net operating income (*NOI*)

One of the first steps in the income capitalization approach is to estimate the potential gross income (*PGI*) of the property. Potential gross income is considered the gross annual income that the subject property could realize assuming 100% occupancy at market rents. *Potential gross income* is the total income attributed to real property at full occupancy before vacancy and operating expenses are deducted.

Because market conditions (demand and supply) vary over time, office properties encounter periods of vacancy. In addition, some tenants may suffer financial setbacks, causing them to miss lease payments or default altogether. Therefore, the operating statement includes a line item to account for *vacancy and collection loss* (V&CL), which is formally defined as

> An allowance for reductions in gross potential income attributable to projected vacancy (physical or economic) and potential collection loss considerations. Vacancy is an expected loss in income as a result of periodic vacant space attributable to unrented space and tenant turnover. Credit loss considers nonpayment of rent and can consider units rented at below-market rates (also known as *lag vacancy*). Vacancy and collection loss is usually estimated on a property-specific basis as part of the reconstructed operating statement in the income capitalization approach and applied, as a percentage, to potential gross income or as a percentage of rentable area of the property; may also refer to a study of vacancy and collection loss in a defined market or submarket.

After deducting for vacancy and collection loss, other income (OI) is added. This results in *effective gross income* (*EGI*), which is the anticipated income from all operations of the real property after an allowance is made for vacancy and collection losses. Effective gross income includes items constituting "other income"–i.e., income generated from the operation of the real property that is not derived from space rental, such as parking rental or income from vending machines.

As noted in the previous definition, *other income* is revenue that comes from a source or sources other than space rental. It can come from a multitude of sources, such as vending machines, parking fees, satellite dishes, helicopter pads, and so on. It can also be revenue that is obtained from a single tenant, such as the leasing of a satellite dish, or revenue that is not associated with any tenant whatsoever, such as vending revenue or public parking fees. Because "other income" is often unique to the subject property, the application of vacancy and collection loss factors must be carefully considered and appropriately applied. In most cases, the estimate of "other income" is the actual revenue anticipated from sources other than space rental; therefore, general vacancy rates are typically not applied to this item.

In short, effective gross income is essentially the estimated cash flow that the owner actually expects to receive. Next, operating expenses (OE) are deducted. *Operating expenses* are the periodic expenditures necessary to maintain the real property and continue production of the effective gross income, assuming prudent and competent management.

Operating expenses are typically segregated between fixed and variable expenses, with occupancy being the distinguishing factor. For instance, property taxes and insurance typically do not vary with occupancy and are therefore considered fixed expenses. However, operating expenses such as maintenance and utilities typically *do* vary with occupancy and are therefore considered variable. Operating expenses typically vary geographically and by property type. Frequently, a property's historical expenses provide the best estimates of its future operating expenses; however, a careful examination of all relevant data leads to the best forecast of operating expenses for the subject property.

The next step is making a deduction for the replacement of short-lived items, referred to as a *replacement allowance* (RES), which is an allowance that provides for the periodic replacement of building components that wear out more rapidly than the building itself and must be replaced during the building's economic life.

The practical application of this particular line item varies considerably, depending on the property type and local practices. However, it is vital that consistency be applied across the comparables and the subject property.

After deducting operating expenses and the replacement allowance from effective gross income, the remainder is labeled *net operating income* (*NOI*), which is the actual or anticipated net income that remains after all operating expenses are deducted from effective gross income but before mortgage debt service and book depreciation are deducted. *NOI* may be calculated before or after deducting replacement reserves.

In the context of office valuation, the conventional operating statement is typically used when valuing the fee simple interest of a stabilized property. Once the net operating income is estimated, market value can be derived by applying a market-derived overall capitalization rate.

Contemporary Operating Statement

Although a conventional operating statement is sufficient in most cases, the format is often less than optimal when valuing the leased fee interest of a multitenant office property with varying lease structures. This is especially the case when the property is not at a stabilized occupancy. In this case, a contemporary operating statement is used, which more accurately identifies the contract and forecast cash flows. An example of this format is provided in Exhibit 5.1.

Multiple periods are provided in Exhibit 5.1, allowing for precise modeling of the anticipated income and expenses over the typical projection period. Within the real estate literature, analysts sometimes refer to the holding period and projection period as being the same. For valuation purposes, however, it is important to carefully distinguish between the two.

A *holding period* is formally defined as "the term of ownership of an investment." A *projection period* is formally defined as "a presumed period of ownership, or a period of time over which expected net operating income is projected for the purposes of analysis and valuation." These formal definitions are important in the valuation of office properties. Even though it might be interesting for an appraiser to know how long a buyer plans to hold or own the property, it really has little relevancy to the valuation. Conversely, the projection period is vitally important to the appraiser. This is the context in which *projection period* will be referred to in the remainder of this text.

Within the commercial real estate industry, five- to 10-year projection periods are frequently used. One might wonder why five- to 10-year periods are used rather than two- to four-year periods or 11- to 15-year

Exhibit 5.1 Sample Annual Operating Statement

Year	1	2	3	4	5	6
Income						
Diamond Wednesday, Inc.						
Rodale Law						
H&B Accounting						
Suite D						
Potential rental income						
Other income						
Expense reimbursements						
Diamond Wednesday, Inc.						
Rodale Law						
H&B Accounting						
Suite D						
Total expense reimbursements						
Total income						
Vacancy allowance						
Effective gross income						
Operating expenses						
Property taxes						
Property insurance						
Property management						
Common area maintenance						
Total operating expenses						
Net operating income						
Leasing commissions						
Tenant improvements						
Capital improvements						
Cash flow before debt service						

Note: Utilities are included with common area maintenance.

periods, for example. Many analysts would claim that a two- to three-year projection period does not give the analyst a clear indication of the future performance of the property and is therefore not enough time. On the other hand, many analysts would claim that attempting to forecast beyond 10 years is too difficult and unreliable. Five to 10 years is considered by many analysts to be the most reasonable projection period.

In the selection of the projection period, the appraiser must survey market participants who are purchasing similar properties in similar locations. Once this projection period is known, the appraiser must carefully consider the term of the existing and forecast leases and ensure that significant events are being considered in the forecast projection; otherwise, important value-influencing events may be inadvertently overlooked.

For example, assume that an appraiser is valuing an office building with a large tenant whose lease will expire in five years. If the appraiser uses a five-year discounted cash flow analysis to value the property, he or she may overlook important data pertaining to this significant lease. In other words, buyers and sellers would include the probable lease terms of this significant tenant beyond the next five years to better calculate and understand the impact it may have on property value. Therefore, the appraiser should carefully consider the typical projection period used by market participants as well as the nuances of the subject property leases when selecting the proper projection period for valuation purposes.

Within this same context, it is important to carefully consider and analyze any vacancy windows that may occur in the subject property. Not all existing tenants renew their lease, and a vacancy window occurs in the analysis when they vacate. If it is uncertain whether an existing tenant is going to renew their lease, the appraiser must estimate the probability of renewal. The appraiser must also estimate the period over which the space will remain vacant until it is re-let. Because of the impact that renewal probability and vacancy may have on the final opinion of value, it is important to carefully analyze each of these factors when employing discounted cash flow analysis for the valuation of the subject property.

Notice the section of the annual operating statement in Exhibit 5.1 that allows expense reimbursements for leases that require the lessee to pay all or part of the operating expenses. In addition, note that the line items for leasing commissions, tenant improvements, and capital improvements are placed below net operating income, resulting in cash flow before debt service. More discussion on these items will be forthcoming.

Reversion Statement

The reversion statement depicts the cash flows realized at the end of the projection period after deducting selling expenses. *Reversion* is a lump-sum benefit that an investor receives or expects to receive at the termination of an investment. It is also known as a *reversionary benefit*.

Depending on the statement and valuation method used, capitalization rates and discount rates are then derived and applied to the applicable cash flows in order to arrive at an estimate of value. A capitalization rate (*R*) is any rate used to convert income into value. A discount rate (*Y*) is an interest rate used to convert future payments or receipts into present value. The discount rate may or may not be the same as the internal rate of return (*IRR*) or yield rate, depending on how it is extracted from the market or used in the analysis.

Discount and Capitalization Rates—Theoretical Relationship

The constant-ratio model provides the basis for the following equation:

$$V = \frac{NOI}{Y_0 - CR}$$

Where

V = property value

NOI = net operating income

Y_0 = free and clear, before-tax yield rate

CR = constant annual growth rate in NOI (periodic compound rate of change)

The basic valuation relationship is:

$$V = \frac{NOI}{R_0}$$

Where

R_0 = overall capitalization rate

Therefore,

$$Y_0 - CR = R_0, \text{ or } Y_0 = R_0 + CR$$

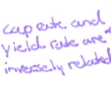

The free and clear, before-tax yield rate is the capitalization rate plus the growth rate. From this, it can be concluded that the capitalization rate will be lower than the yield rate when income is expected to increase. When income is expected to decrease, the capitalization rate will be higher than the yield rate. When income is expected to remain constant, the capitalization rate (sometimes shortened to *cap rate*) and yield rate will converge. These relationships are illustrated in the following table:

	future **increases** in income & expenses		the capitalization rate will be **lower** than the discount rate
If the market's expectation is for	**stable** income & value	**then**	the capitalization rate & discount rate will **converge**—i.e., be the same
	future **declines** in income & value		the capitalization rate will be **higher** than the discount rate

In addition to understanding the relationship between capitalization rates and yield rates, it is important to consider the relationship between rates that are applied to different interests of the property being appraised. For instance, consider the following:

$$Y_{LF} < Y_0 < Y_{LH}$$
$$R_{LF} < R_0 < R_{LH},$$

Where

Y_{LF} = leased fee, free and clear, before-tax yield rate

Y_O = fee simple, free and clear, before-tax yield rate

Y_{LH} = leasehold, free and clear, before-tax yield rate

R_{LF} = leased fee capitalization rate

R_O = fee simple capitalization rate

R_{LH} = leasehold capitalization rate

These relationships reflect typical risk differentials between various interests in the property. In the valuation of the subject property, it is important to adequately address these relationships and explain any deviations. For instance, properties with below-market rents typically have capitalization and yield rates that are less than the fee simple capitalization and yield rates. This is because the leased fee position is a more secure investment opportunity due to the below-market rents and tenants will probably stay in the property because they are receiving a benefit. So, in short, there are a multitude of rates that may be used for a property depending on the income status and whether or not contract rent is the same as market rent.

Section 2. Office Leases and Important Terms

Office leases are generally separated either by the treatment of operating expenses or by rent provisions, as shown in Exhibit 5.2.

The leases depicted by treatment of expenses in Exhibit 5.2 are bookended by the gross and absolute net leases. A gross lease calls for the owner or lessor to pay *all* operating expenses, while the absolute net lease calls for the tenant or lessee to pay for *all* operating expenses. The *net*, the *net net* (double net), and the *net net net* (triple net) leases are combinations of the gross and absolute net leases. Even though the *Dictionary of Real Estate Appraisal* provides formal definitions of all of these types of leases, interpretations of these definitions vary geographically. As a result, it is essential that the appraiser understand the local criteria and carefully define and consistently apply these criteria in the appraisal report.

Leases that are categorized by rent provisions–escalator leases, flat rental leases, graduated rental leases, index leases, percentage leases,

Exhibit 5.2 Lease Types

By Treatment of Expenses	By Rent Provisions
❑ Gross lease	❑ Escalator lease
❑ Net lease	❑ Flat rental lease
❑ Net net lease	❑ Graduated rental lease
❑ Net net net lease	❑ Index lease
❑ Absolute net lease	❑ Percentage lease
	❑ Revaluation lease

and revaluation leases–are interpreted and applied more consistently across geographic areas and property types. An *escalator lease* allows for the lessor to seek reimbursement of operating expenses after specific criteria have been met. For instance, an office lease may call for the lessor to pay all operating expenses the first year, with the lessee reimbursing the lessor for all operating expenses that exceed the first year's expenses in subsequent years. This arrangement is referred to as a *base-year expense stop*. Similarly, the lessor and lessee may negotiate a specific dollar expense stop, which provides for the lessee to reimburse the lessor for all operating expenses exceeding a specified dollar amount.

A *flat rental lease* stipulates that the rental rate will remain fixed for the term of the lease. These leases are typically written for short periods during soft market conditions, which allows the lessor to renegotiate the lease once market conditions have improved. A *graduated rental lease*, sometimes referred to as a *step lease*, stipulates that the rental rate will change by an agreed amount at precise periods in the term of the lease. For instance, the lease may state that rents increase one dollar per square foot on the lease's annual anniversary over the term of the lease. An *index lease* ties the rental rate to a financial or economic index, such as the consumer price index (CPI). This type of lease typically requires a periodic adjustment (such as an annual adjustment) according to changes in the CPI. The primary intent of this type of lease is to protect the lessor from inflation risk, especially if the lease is written for a long term. A *percentage lease* is typically associated with retail tenants and requires that the tenant pay the landlord an agreed-upon percentage of gross sales in addition to a base rental rate. In the context of office valuation, retail tenants frequently occupy ground-level space, especially in office properties located in a CBD. Percentage leases exist to provide an incentive for the lessor/landlord to do everything possible to encourage patrons to frequent the retail business. A *revaluation lease* is typically a long-term lease that requires a fresh look at market conditions at the time of renewal. In this case, the lease may stipulate that an MAI-designated appraiser be retained by both parties to research market conditions and estimate a market rental rate on the tenant's space, thereby allowing the lease rates to return to market levels.

Important Elements in Lease Contracts

Lease contracts are typically written by attorneys who try to anticipate potential problems and ensure that the client is adequately protected. Therefore, the sheer volume of legal verbiage can sometimes overwhelm the appraiser. The appraiser must be careful to focus on the elements in the lease contract that may influence property value, including the following:

- Identification of the lessor (landlord) and lessee (tenant)
- Type of tenant
- Description of leased premises

- Term of lease
- Lease payment and/or method of calculation
- Operating expense responsibility
- Tenant improvements
- Renewal options
- Sublease options

Office property owners typically use a master lease that is slightly modified for each tenant. On a practical basis, the appraiser can first focus on the master lease and identify the important elements that may influence property value. Once this has been done, the appraiser can then design and populate a lease abstract that summarizes important lease data for each lease in the subject property. Exhibit 5.3 provides an example of a lease abstract form that may be completed by the appraiser.

Exhibit 5.3 Sample Lease Abstract

Lease number: ____________________

Tenant name: ____________________

Suite number: ____________________

Date lease began: ____________________

Date lease ends: ____________________

Rentable square feet: ____________________

Usable square feet: ____________________

Current annual rent: ____________________

Rent escalations: ____________________

Operating expense agreements: ____________________

Renewal rents/provisions: ____________________

Renewal probability: ____________________

Tenant improvements: ____________________

At commencement: ____________________

At renewal: ____________________

Leasing commissions: ____________________

At commencement: ____________________

At renewal: ____________________

Once a lease abstract has been generated for each tenant, the appraiser must begin to analyze each lease. The analysis may include carefully assessing the creditworthiness of the tenant (i.e., the probability that the tenant will actually perform according to the terms of the contract), calculating the contract rental revenue over the term of the contract, examining renewal clauses and estimating the probability of renewal, calculating operating expense reimbursements based on operating expense agreements, and identifying and estimating tenant improvement allowances and leasing commissions.

Section 3. Maple Landing Case Study

Introduction

The previous two sections of this chapter provided the theoretical and terminological foundation for the remainder of this chapter. The office building valuation case study presented here has been included to provide a practical application of the income capitalization approach for a stabilized multitenant office building with varying lease structures.

Overview

The subject property, Maple Landing, is a 30,000-sq.-ft., three-story office/retail building. There are 10,000 square feet of floor-rentable area on each level. At street grade, the first level has 4,500 square feet allocated to a retail tenant, while the remainder of the building is designated as office space. The building was originally constructed in 1979 and underwent a major renovation about two years ago. Currently, there are three tenants occupying the building, each with different lease terms.

Tenants

Diamond Wednesday, Inc.	· Restaurant tenant · Located on the first floor · Occupies 4,500 square feet of rentable area · Moved in shortly after renovation two years ago · Will pay $19.50 per square foot next year on a net lease basis, fixed, for 10 years · Has the right to renew for another 10 years at market rent
Rodale Law	· Occupies 5,500 square feet of rentable area on the first floor and 10,000 square feet of rentable area on the second floor · Has experienced considerable growth over the past 10 years and moved to the subject property in order to accommodate this expansion · Lease began two years ago and has a term of 10 years with an option to renew at market rates · Will pay rent of $15.75 per square foot the next year, with an expense stop of $4.25 · Lease calls for the rent to escalate at 2% per year thereafter
H&B Accounting	· Occupies 7,600 square feet of rentable area on the third floor · Will pay $17.00 per square foot per year over the next 12 months on a full-service basis · Escalation clause provides for a 3.5% increase in rent per year over the five-year term of the lease, which began two years ago

	• Will exercise their option to renew for another five years at a fixed rent of $20 per square foot per year, full service • At the time of renewal, the owner will give the lessee a tenant improvement allowance of $4 per square foot to refresh the space • Leasing commissions at the time of renewal are estimated at 2%, paid up front
Suite D	• Takes up remainder of building space, which is 2,400 square feet of rentable area on the third floor • Has just been leased at $16.00 per square foot per year, with rents escalating at 3.5% per year and an expense stop of $5.00 per square foot • Lease term is seven years • For this new tenant, the tenant improvement allowance is $12.00 per square foot, and the leasing commission is 4%, paid during the first month

Operating Expenses

- Property taxes are $64,000, paid at the end of the year.
- Property insurance is $0.23 per square foot of rentable area per year.
- Property management is 4% of contract rental revenue.
- Common area maintenance is $3.25 per square foot of rentable area per year.
- Property taxes are expected to increase by 4% per year, while insurance and common area maintenance are expected to increase by 3% per year over the next 10 years.

Capital Expenditures

At the time of renovation, the owners elected to postpone the replacement of the roof. However, all parties agree that a capital expenditure of $40,000 will be required in four years to replace the roof.

Other Research

Research shows that investors allocate a minimum vacancy of at least 5%, even when a property is fully occupied. In addition, research finds that contemporary capitalization rates for similar buildings are 8.5%, reversionary capitalization rates are about 25 basis points higher, a five-year projection period is most commonly used for analysis purposes, and selling expenses are about 5%. Research also finds that investors are using an approximate 10% discount rate when discounting the cash flows before debt service and the reversion to arrive at a value estimate. Research finds that market participants are not deducting replacement reserves prior to calculating net operating income, but they are deducting leasing fees and capital expenses prior to calculating cash flow before debt service.

Supporting each of these inputs requires careful attention to the methods and data used by market participants. Some of these inputs may be obtained from conversations with buyers and sellers in the confirmation of comparable sales or from actual market transactions. Examples include the typical projection period, capitalization rates, yield rates, and the application of reserves. Other inputs such as selling expenses may be obtained from local brokers or third-party data providers. Whatever method is used, it is incumbent upon the appraiser to conduct the necessary research to ensure that the inputs are reliable and supported by the market. This may require extensive research and analysis that should not be underestimated. On a practical basis, many appraisers maintain files that include transaction details and written records of conversations with market participants in an effort to support these important valuation inputs.

Section 4. Estimating Rents and Vacancies

Estimating the subject property's future rental revenue and vacancy is a two-step process. First, the appraiser estimates the subject property's contract rents and vacancies by evaluating the creditworthiness of each tenant, identifying and calculating the contract rents over the holding period (including agreed-upon escalations in rent), identifying renewal clauses, and determining the probability of renewal. Second, the appraiser estimates market rents and vacancies by completing a competitive market analysis.

Estimating Contract Rents and Vacancies

Office property investors carefully examine the creditworthiness of existing tenants to gauge the riskiness of the future cash flows, so appraisers must also carefully evaluate each tenant's creditworthiness. The rent payment history and the ownership structure can provide insight into the stability of a tenant. For instance, a public corporation may have financial statements that are publicly available, which can help the appraiser gauge the financial health of the firm. For closely held corporations, an assessment of firm longevity and local reputation may provide insight into creditworthiness. In addition, personal guarantees by the principals of the firm may increase the strength of the lease. In short, the ability to estimate creditworthiness is an important part of appraising multitenant office properties. Appraisers with less experience should seek assistance from more experienced appraisers, if needed, to adequately assess the risk in the existing tenant rent roll.

Next, the appraiser actually forecasts the potential gross income for each tenant by examining the abstracts generated from the lease contracts. For illustrative purposes, the potential gross income is forecast for each of the leases in the Maple Landing office/retail property.

Maple Landing Case Study: Forecasting Rental Income for Existing Tenants

Diamond Wednesday, Inc., Contract Terms

- Creditworthiness: High (national credit tenant)
- Usable square feet: 4,018
- Load factor: 12%
- Rentable square feet: 4,500
- Term of lease: 10 years (began 2 years ago)
- Escalation clauses: None
- Renewal clauses: Right to renew for another 10 years at market rate
- Contract/forecast rents: $19.50 per square foot per year (rentable)

Year	1	2	3	4	5	6
Rental income	$87,750	$87,750	$87,750	$87,750	$87,750	$87,750

Rodale Law Contract Terms

- Creditworthiness: Good
- Usable square feet: 13,840
- Load factor: 12%
- Rentable square feet: 15,500
- Term of lease: 10 years (began 2 years ago)
- Escalation clauses: 2% annually
- Renewal clauses: Right to renew at market rate
- Contract/forecast rents: $15.75 per square foot per year (rentable)

Year	1	2	3	4	5	6
Rental income	$244,125	$249,008	$253,988	$259,067	$264,249	$269,534

H&B Accounting Contract Terms

- Creditworthiness: Average
- Usable square feet: 6,786
- Load factor: 12%
- Rentable square feet: 7,600
- Term of lease: 5 years (began 2 years ago)
- Escalation clauses: 3.5% annually
- Renewal clauses: Right to renew for 5 additional years at $20 per square foot per year, fixed
- Contract/forecast rents: 3 years at $17 per square foot per year, 5 years at $20 square foot per year (rentable)

Year	1	2	3	4	5	6
Rental income	$129,200	$133,722	$138,402	$152,000	$152,000	$152,000

Suite D Contract Terms

- Creditworthiness: Average
- Usable square feet: 2,143
- Load factor: 12%
- Rentable square feet: 2,400
- Term of lease: 7 years
- Escalation clauses: 3.5% annually
- Renewal clauses: None
- Contract/forecast rents: $16 per square foot per year (rentable)

Year	1	2	3	4	5	6
Rental income	$38,400	$39,744	$41,135	$42,575	$44,065	$45,607

Exhibit 5.4 Summary of Contract Rental Revenue Forecast

Year	1	2	3	4	5	6
Income						
Diamond Wednesday, Inc.	$87,750	$87,750	$87,750	$87,750	$87,750	$87,750
Rodale Law	$244,125	$249,008	$253,988	$259,067	$264,249	$269,534
H&B Accounting	$129,200	$133,722	$138,402	$152,000	$152,000	$152,000
Suite D	$38,400	$39,744	$41,135	$42,575	$44,065	$45,607
Potential rental income	$499,475	$510,224	$521,275	$541,392	$548,064	$554,891
Other income						
Expense reimbursements						
Diamond Wednesday, Inc.						
Rodale Law						
H&B Accounting						
Suite D						
Total expense reimbursements						
Total income						
Vacancy allowance 5%						
Effective gross income						
Operating expenses						
Property taxes						
Property insurance						
Property management						
Common area maintenance						
Total operating expenses						
Net operating income						
Leasing commissions						
Tenant improvements						
Capital improvements						
Cash flow before debt service						

Estimating Market Rents and Vacancies

Market rent is defined as the most probable rent that a property should bring in a competitive and open market, reflecting all conditions and restrictions of the typical lease agreement, including the rental adjustment and revaluation, term, permitted uses, use restrictions, expense obligations, concessions, renewal and purchase options, and tenant improvements (TIs).[2]

Estimating market rents and vacancies for the subject property is accomplished by examining current rental data from the subject property, nearby competing properties, and secondary data providers. Data compiled firsthand is referred to as *primary data* and is typically given greater weight than other data sources because the appraiser can more easily assess its reliability. To gather primary data, the appraiser typically creates a short list of competing and comparable properties, including the subject property. After carefully designing a survey form like the one shown in Exhibit 5.5, the appraiser contacts the owners, managers, and brokers of the comparable properties.

survey form

The appraiser consistently questions these individuals in an effort to ascertain the rent and occupancy data from these competing properties. This process requires finesse and experience because market participants are often apprehensive to share this data. Preparation and organization are essential for successfully obtaining this information. The appraiser should obtain all publicly available data regarding the property and become familiar with its physical characteristics prior to making contact with these individuals. It is also helpful for the appraiser to review any secondary data regarding the property that may be available from other sources. When preparing for the conversation, it is wise to avoid questions with little relevancy to the objective or for which the answers are readily available from an on-site inspection or public records. It is also imperative that the appraiser not disclose confidential information.

When the appraiser has done enough background research and is prepared and sensitive to the respondent's time, the conversation typically goes much more smoothly and the respondent is much more willing to confirm and convey information critical to the valuation process. Analysis of this primary data generally provides the best support for estimating the market rents and vacancy rates for the subject property.

To support and verify the reasonableness of the primary data, secondary rental and occupancy data can be obtained from national organizations such as BOMA International or the Institute of Real Estate Management (IREM), as well as local third-party data providers.

Secondary data is information from secondary sources, meaning that it is not directly compiled by the analyst. Secondary data may include any published or unpublished work based on research that relies on

---

2. *The Appraisal of Real Estate*, 13th ed. (Chicago: Appraisal Institute, 2008), 453.

Exhibit 5.5 | Sample Office Rent Survey Form

Building Information

Name: ______________________________

Address: ______________________________

Square feet (gross): ______________________________

Square feet (rentable): ______________________________

Square feet (usable): ______________________________

Load factor: ______________________________

Efficiency ratio: ______________________________

Rental rate range: ______________________________

Vacancy rate: ______________________________

Number of parking spaces: ______________________________

Common area finish:	high	average	low

Tenant Information

Name: ______________________________

Address/suite number: ______________________________

Square feet (usable): ______________________________

Lease type:	gross	net	hybrid

Rental rate (per sq. ft. per year): ______________________________

Lease term (years): ______________________________

Tenant improvement allowance (price per sq. ft.): ______________________________

Leasing commission: ______________________________

Tenant finish:	high	average	low
HVAC:	high	average	low
Security:	high	average	low
Technology:	high	average	low
Parking satisfaction:	high	average	low

Number of employees: ______________________________

Square foot per employee: ______________________________

Comments: ______________________________

primary sources or any material other than primary sources used to prepare a written work.

Secondary data provides a broader perspective of rents and vacancies and allows the analyst to benchmark primary research findings against a larger and broader sample. Exhibit 5.6 provides a sample of secondary data obtained from BOMA.

The income categories shown in Exhibit 5.6 include office area rent, retail area rent, "other area" rent, parking income, tenant services, and "miscellaneous." BOMA reports the number of member buildings included in the report, the total square feet of space, and the average rental rate, as well as the minimum and maximum statistics for each category. This data can provide secondary support for the conclusion of market rent and occupancy for the subject property.

Exhibit 5.6 Sample BOMA Office Income and Expense Survey

Phoenix, AZ

ALL SUBURBAN

INCOME	# BLDS	Total Building Rentable Area (48 BLDS, 5,069,749 SQ. FT.) Dollars/Sq. Ft. AVG	MEDIAN	Mid Range** LOW	HIGH	Total Office Rentable Area (5,069,749 SQ. FT.) Dollars/Sq. Ft. AVG	MEDIAN	Mid Range** LOW	HIGH
OFFICE AREA	42					16.94	16.60	10.51	18.71
RETAIL AREA									
OTHER AREA									
TOTAL RENT	42	17.15	17.63	10.51	20.03				
GROSS PARKING INC	28	.40	.10	.05	.20				
TENANT SERVICES	4	.22	.10						
MISCELLANEOUS	19	.31	.08	.03	.14				
TOTAL INCOME	42	17.58	18.18	10.51	20.12				
EXPENSE									
CLEANING	18	.97	.95	.75	1.11	.97	.95	.75	1.11
REPAIR/MAINT	23	1.05	.92	.83	1.24	1.05	.92	.83	1.24
UTILITIES	29	1.82	1.79	1.54	1.99	1.82	1.79	1.54	1.99
ROADS/GROUNDS	47	.16	.25	.19	.40	.16	.25	.19	.40
SECURITY	21	.17	.15	.09	.40	.17	.15	.09	.40
ADMINISTRATIVE	47	.58	.77	.54	1.22	.58	.77	.54	1.22
TOTAL OPER EXP	40	4.79	4.66	2.93	5.49	4.79	4.66	2.93	5.49
FIXED EXPENSE	46	1.36	2.40	1.88	2.69	1.36	2.40	1.88	2.69
TOTAL OPER+FIX	42	6.84	6.75	3.63	8.06	6.84	6.75	3.63	8.06
DIR LEASING EXP	17	.94	.20	.13	.66	.94	.20	.13	.66
AMORT LEASING EXP	6	.84	.99	.66	1.45	.84	.99	.66	1.45
PARKING EXP									

OCCUPANCY INFO.	AVERAGE	BLDS
SQFT/OFFICE TENANT	14719.80	46
SQFT/RETAIL TENANT		
SQFT/OFFICE WORKER	673.31	25
SQFT/MAINTENANCE STAFF	109147.71	25
OFFICE OCCUPANCY (%)	94.46	35
RETAIL OCCUPANCY (%)		
YR-END RENT ($)	20.35	29
GROSS PARKING INC/STALL ($)	110.23	23
PARKING RATIO (STALLS/1000SF)	3.84	25
RENTABLE/GROSS SQFT	.98	27
RENTABLE/USABLE SQFT	1.06	22
TOTAL BTUs		
CAPITALIZATION THRESHOLD ($)	7200.00	5
BUILDING HOURS	77.42	40

DETAIL*	AVERAGE	BLDS
OFFICE RENT		
BASE RENT	15.62	40
PASS-THROUGHS	2.51	23
OPER COST ESCAL	1.06	10
BASE RENT ESCAL		
LEASE CANCEL	.17	2
RENT ABATEMENT		
CLEANING		
PAYROLL		
ROUTINE CONTRACT	.65	16
SPEC CONTRACT	.04	45
SUP/MAT/MISC	.06	27
TRASH REMOVAL	.04	40
REPAIR/MAINT		
PAYROLL	.13	21

DETAIL*	AVERAGE	BLDS
ELEVATOR	.03	20
HVAC	.10	34
ELECTRICAL	.02	41
STRUC/ROOF	.20	35
PLUMBING	.01	34
FIRE/LIFE SAFETY	.03	43
GEN EXTERIOR	.05	43
GEN INTERIOR	.08	44
CONTRACT	.30	2
UTILITIES		
ELECTRICITY	1.66	29
GAS	.04	12
FUEL OIL		
STEAM		
CH WTR		
WATER/SEWER	.13	43

DETAIL*	AVERAGE	BLDS
RDS/GDS		
RDS/GDS LANDSCAPE	.13	46
RDS/GDS GARAGE	.02	40
RDS/GDS SNOW		
RDS/GDS OTHER	.04	18
SEC		
SEC PAYROLL		
SEC CONTRACT	.14	23
SEC EQUIPMENT		
SEC OTHER	.05	4
ADMINISTRATIVE		
PAYROLL	.14	15
ALLOC ADMIN		
MGMT FEES	.38	46
PROF FEES	.05	17

DETAIL*	AVERAGE	BLDS
GEN OFC EXP	.05	18
EMP EXP		
OTHER ADM EXP	.04	13
FIXED EXPENSES		
REAL ESTATE TAX	1.27	46
BLDG INSURANCE	.08	42
PERS PROP TAX		
OTHER TAX		
LICENSE FEE	.18	11
LEASING EXPENSES		
PAYROLL		
ADV/PROMOTION	.03	16
TRAVEL	.13	3
DIR-COMMISSIONS	.58	11
DIR-BUY OUT		
PROF FEES	.05	11

DETAIL*	AVERAGE	BLDS
DIR-TENANT IMP	1.16	5
DIR-OTHER	.01	10
AMORT-COMMISION	.53	6
AMORT-TENANT IMP	.39	5
AMORT-BUY-OUTS		
AMORT-OTHER		
PARKING		
IN HOUSE		
CONTRACT		
SNOW		
SHUTTLE		
TELECOMMUNICATIONS		
WIRE ACCESS		
ROOF TOP	.02	2
TOTAL INCOME	.02	2
TOTAL EXPENSES		

*Income calculation based on office rentable sq. ft.; Expense calculation based on total bldg. rentable sq. ft.
**low = 25th percentile; high = 75th percentile

Source: BOMA International. Used with permission.

IREM also provides secondary rental and occupancy data. IREM is an affiliate of the National Association of Realtors. IREM surveys nearly 2,500 private-sector office buildings in major metropolitan and suburban markets. The data includes over 50 specific categories and is arranged by building size, height, age, and rental range. The report provides revenue and vacancy data as well as data on operating expenses and leasing commissions. Exhibit 5.7 provides a sample of IREM data.

Other Income

For the most part, other income is a minor revenue line item, and the practical cost of researching comparable data may not be justified. On the other hand, an improvement such as a parking garage that generates significant revenue may warrant considerable market research to adequately forecast revenue. For the Maple Landing Case Study property, no other income was noted.

Section 5. Operating Expenses, Leasing Commissions, and Capital Costs

Operating expenses are typically allocated between fixed and variable expenses. Fixed operating expenses do not vary with occupancy and may include items such as property taxes and insurance. Variable operating expenses vary with occupancy and may include items such

Exhibit 5.7 Sample IREM Office Income and Expense Data

SELECTED METROPOLITAN AREAS DOWNTOWN

DOWNTOWN OFFICE BUILDINGS — METROPOLITAN DALLAS, TX

CHART OF ACCOUNTS	$/GROSS AREA OF ENTIRE BLG.					$/GROSS RENTABLE OFFC. AREA					$/NET RENTABLE OFFC. AREA				
	BLGS	SQ. FT. (10000)	$ MED.	$ RANGE LOW	$ RANGE HIGH	BLGS	SQ. FT. (10000)	$ MED.	$ RANGE LOW	$ RANGE HIGH	BLGS	SQ. FT. (10000)	$ MED.	$ RANGE LOW	$ RANGE HIGH
INCOME															
OFFICES	14	1388	12.21	10.83	14.27	14	1274	13.46	12.20	14.52	14	1210	14.27	13.00	15.79
RETAIL	8	894	.09	.04	.10	8	805	.09	.05	.12	8	760	.09	.06	.12
PARKING	9	955	.97	.49	1.06	9	869	1.01	.57	1.07	9	830	1.06	.57	1.17
OTHER	4	593	.19	.02	.19	4	509	.21	.03	.21	4	472	.23	.03	.23
PASS-THROUGHS	9	912	1.74	1.16	2.22	9	818	2.00	1.30	2.42	9	754	2.00	1.41	2.52
RETAIL % INCOME	2	376	.04	.02	.04	2	358	.05	.02	.05	2	343	.05	.02	.05
MISC. INCOME	12	1224	.35	.13	.45	12	1127	.40	.14	.45	12	1073	.40	.14	.45
VACANCY/DELIN. RENTS	10	1194	2.99	2.00	3.92	10	1084	3.53	2.13	4.30	10	1020	3.64	2.46	4.66
TOTAL COLLECTIONS	14	1388	16.95	13.18	18.21	14	1274	17.57	15.61	20.15	14	1210	17.57	16.29	21.26
EXPENSES															
ELECTRICITY	5	403	.69	.51	.87	5	383	.69	.51	.87	5	380	.69	.51	.87
WATER & SEWER	16	1540	.09	.06	.11	16	1385	.09	.07	.13	16	1332	.10	.07	.13
HVAC FUEL															
GAS	4	227	.23	.06	.23	4	201	.23	.07	.23	4	201	.23	.07	.23
FUEL OIL															
ELECTRICITY	17	1630	1.63	1.39	2.02	17	1468	2.07	1.58	2.25	17	1411	2.11	1.58	2.45
STEAM															
OTHER															
COMBINATION ELECTRIC	5	403	1.89	1.72	2.17	5	383	1.89	1.73	2.17	5	380	1.89	1.72	2.17
SUBTOTAL UTILITIES	17	1630	2.12	1.92	2.46	17	1468	2.33	2.14	2.71	17	1411	2.47	2.20	2.98
JANITORIAL															
PAYROLL/CONTRACT	17	1630	.62	.53	.73	17	1468	.66	.58	.77	17	1411	.70	.62	.77
SUPPLIES	8	951	.07	.04	.08	8	871	.08	.06	.08	8	822	.08	.07	.09
MISCELLANEOUS	6	750	.03	.01	.03	6	673	.04	.01	.04	6	655	.04	.02	.04
MAINT. & REPAIR															
PAYROLL	16	1615	.37	.33	.53	16	1454	.42	.35	.53	16	1399	.42	.35	.55
HTG/VEN & AC REPAIRS	17	1630	.14	.11	.17	17	1468	.15	.11	.20	17	1411	.17	.11	.23
ELECTRIC REPAIRS	17	1630	.04	.03	.07	17	1468	.04	.03	.08	17	1411	.05	.03	.09
PLUMBING REPAIRS	17	1630	.03	.02	.04	17	1468	.03	.02	.04	17	1411	.03	.02	.04
ELEV REPR/MAINT.	17	1630	.19	.17	.35	17	1468	.25	.19	.38	17	1411	.28	.19	.36
GENERAL BUILDING EXTER.	17	1630	.03	.01	.11	17	1468	.03	.02	.11	17	1411	.03	.02	.12
ROOF REPAIRS	10	1115	.01	.00	.02	10	1012	.01	.00	.02	10	971	.01	.00	.02
PARKING LOT REPAIRS	7	395	.02	.01	.03	7	349	.02	.01	.04	7	338	.02	.01	.04
GENERAL BUILDING INTER.	17	1630	.10	.05	.13	17	1468	.10	.06	.18	17	1411	.10	.06	.20
MISC. REPAIRS	15	1497	.05	.03	.06	15	1369	.06	.03	.07	15	1321	.06	.03	.07
SUBTOTAL JAN/MAIN/RPR	17	1630	1.64	1.49	2.03	17	1468	1.81	1.73	2.24	17	1411	1.87	1.82	2.46
ADMINISTRATIVE															
PAYROLL-ADMINIST.	17	1630	.39	.29	.45	17	1468	.42	.29	.47	17	1411	.46	.29	.48
ADVERTISING	9	1068	.03	.02	.07	9	966	.04	.03	.07	9	913	.04	.03	.08
MANAGEMENT FEE	17	1630	.37	.25	.42	17	1468	.39	.27	.51	17	1411	.41	.27	.59
OTHER ADMINISTRATIVE	17	1630	.24	.16	.30	17	1468	.26	.16	.36	17	1411	.30	.17	.38
SUBTOTAL ADMIN/PAYROLL	17	1630	1.03	.90	1.26	17	1468	1.15	.96	1.43	17	1411	1.25	.96	1.53
SERVICES															
LANDSCAPE	17	1630	.06	.02	.09	17	1468	.07	.02	.10	17	1411	.07	.02	.11
TRASH REMOVAL	17	1630	.02	.02	.03	17	1468	.03	.02	.03	17	1411	.03	.02	.04
SECURITY-PAYROLL	8	664	.47	.29	.54	8	604	.51	.29	.61	8	581	.53	.29	.61
SECURITY-CONTRACTED	14	1327	.57	.42	.71	14	1224	.59	.45	.75	14	1161	.68	.46	.82
WINDOWS WASHING	17	1630	.02	.02	.05	17	1468	.02	.02	.05	17	1411	.02	.02	.05
SNOW REMOVAL	2	181	.00			2	177	.00			2	168	.00		
MISCELLANEOUS	3	194	.01	.00	.01	3	188	.01	.00	.01	3	175	.01	.00	.01
SUBTOTAL SERVICES	17	1630	1.03	.86	1.24	17	1468	1.11	.92	1.25	17	1411	1.16	.94	1.26
NET OPERATING COSTS	17	1630	6.15	5.42	6.71	17	1468	6.51	5.90	7.15	17	1411	6.96	6.40	7.85
INSURANCE	17	1630	.22	.16	.31	17	1468	.24	.16	.32	17	1411	.26	.16	.33
REAL ESTATE TAXES	17	1630	1.61	1.16	2.45	17	1468	1.95	1.32	2.66	17	1411	2.02	1.32	2.66
OTHER TAX/FEE/PERMIT	8	858	.01	.01	.03	8	786	.01	.01	.04	8	742	.01	.01	.04
TOTAL OPERATING COSTS	17	1630	7.88	7.20	9.24	17	1468	8.95	7.66	9.48	17	1411	8.95	8.42	10.29

OCCUPANCY LEVEL	82%	E/I RATIO (TOC/TAC)	.54	TENANTS	3-YEAR	(6)	$10.00
VACANCY LEVEL	18%	CLEANING SERVICES (% YES)	18%	ALTERATIONS	5-YEAR	(7)	$15.00

FOOTNOTE: SQUARE FOOTAGE FIGURES (SQ.FT.) ARE REPORTED IN MULTIPLES OF TEN THOUSAND. SEE GUIDELINES SECTION FOR EXPLANATION OF REPORTS AND INTERPRETATION OF DATA. COPYRIGHT 2006, IREM

Source: IREM. Used with permission.

as cleaning and janitorial services, repairs and maintenance, utilities, landscaping, grounds and road maintenance, security, and management and administration. Operating expenses may vary considerably based on property type and geographic location. Primary research generally provides the best estimates for operating expenses. The operating expense history of the subject property should be carefully examined and benchmarked with competing properties and third-party data providers. BOMA provides summaries of operating expenses in most major metropolitan areas by office property type. Exhibit 5.6 provides sample BOMA operating expense data.

In addition to the aggregate operating expenses observed in the center portion of Exhibit 5.6, BOMA also provides detailed data pertaining to each of the operating expense categories. This data may be helpful in providing the appraiser with an additional resource to estimate operating expenses for the subject property. In fact, the operating expense data provided by BOMA is often considered to be more beneficial to the appraiser than rental data because operating expense comparables are typically more difficult to obtain. Since the estimated operating expenses can have a significant impact on net operating income and the overall estimate of value, it is imperative that the appraiser perform a careful examination of third-party data.

After estimating the overall operating expenses for the subject property, the appraiser then determines who is responsible for the payment. Operating expense lease clauses stipulate whether the landlord, tenant, or both are responsible for the operating expenses. An expense stop requires that the tenant reimburse the landlord for any operating expense over the stop (base year or dollar amount). The following example shows how expense stops are calculated.

Example of Expense Stop Calculation

The marketing firm of Harry & Harry signed a lease with an expense stop based on the base-year operating expenses. The lease is for 3,000 square feet within a building of 62,000 total square feet. The tenant is responsible for the pro rata share of any increase. Base-year expenses totaled $294,500, and expenses in the second year increased to $306,000.

Sample Exercises

1. What percentage of the building does the tenant occupy?

   Answer: $$\frac{3{,}000}{62{,}000} = 4.839\%$$

2. What is the total increase in expenses for the building?

   Answer: $306,000 – $294,500 = $11,500

3. What is the additional amount the tenant must pay as a result of increased expenses?

   Answer: $11,500 × 0.04839 = $556.49

4. What are the indicated base-year expenses on a per-square-foot basis?

   Answer: $294,500 / 62,000 = $4.75

5. What are the second-year expenses on a per-square-foot basis?

   Answer: $306,000 / 62,000 = $4.935

6. What is the percentage increase in expenses?

   Answer: $$\frac{4.935 - 4.75}{4.75} = 3.9\%$$

Maple Landing Case Study: Operating Expense Forecast

The Maple Landing Case Study provides the following estimates of future operating expenses:

1. Property taxes are $64,000, due at the end of the year.
2. Property insurance is $0.23 per square foot of rentable area per year.
3. Property management is 4% of collected rental revenue.
4. Common area maintenance is $3.25 per square foot of rentable area per year.
5. Property taxes are forecast to increase 4% per year while insurance and common area maintenance are expected to increase 3% per year over the next 10 years.

Based on this data, operating expenses are forecast over the holding period as shown in Exhibit 5.8.

Some of the leases in the Maple Landing Case Study stipulated that the tenant would reimburse the landlord under certain conditions. As a result, the lease terms for each tenant must be reviewed to determine if reimbursements are required and to estimate the amount of the reimbursement, if warranted. The following example illustrates this process for each tenant in the Maple Landing Case Study.

Forecasting Operating Expense Reimbursements Over Projection Holding Period

Diamond Wednesday, Inc., Contract

- Operating expense terms: Absolute net lease
- Reimbursements

Year	**1**	**2**	**3**	**4**	**5**	**6**
Expense reimbursements	$28,257	$29,175	$30,125	$31,159	$32,144	$33,163

For the first year, the reimbursement amount is calculated by first dividing the rentable area of Diamond Wednesday (4,500 square feet) by the building rentable area (30,000 square feet) to calculate the pro rata share of rentable area (15%). Since Diamond Wednesday has an absolute net lease, they are responsible for their full pro rata share of the total operating expenses ($188,379), which results in a reimbursement of $28,257 (0.15 × $188,379). This same procedure can be applied to the total operating expense estimates in subsequent years to calculate the reimbursement amount for each year.

Exhibit 5.8 Maple Landing Operating Expense Forecast						
Year	**1**	**2**	**3**	**4**	**5**	**6**
Income						
Diamond Wednesday, Inc.	$87,750	$87,750	$87,750	$87,750	$87,750	$87,750
Rodale Law	$244,125	$249,008	$253,988	$259,067	$264,249	$269,534
H&B Accounting	$129,200	$133,722	$138,402	$152,000	$152,000	$152,000
Suite D	$38,400	$39,744	$41,135	$42,575	$44,065	$45,607
Potential rental income	$499,475	$510,224	$521,275	$541,392	$548,064	$554,891
Other income						
Expense reimbursements						
Diamond Wednesday, Inc.						
Rodale Law						
H&B Accounting						
Suite D						
Total expense reimbursements						
Total income						
Vacancy allowance 5%						
Effective gross income						
Operating expenses						
Property taxes	$64,000	$66,560	$69,222	$71,991	$74,871	$77,866
Property insurance	$6,900	$7,107	$7,320	$7,540	$7,766	$7,999
Property management	$19,979	$20,409	$20,851	$21,656	$21,923	$22,196
Common area maintenance	$97,500	$100,425	$103,438	$106,541	$109,737	$113,029
Total operating expenses	$188,379	$194,501	$200,831	$207,728	$214,297	$221,090
Net operating income						
Leasing commissions						
Tenant improvements						
Capital improvements						
Cash flow before debt service						

Rodale Law Contract

- Operating expense terms: $4.25 per square foot expense stop
- Reimbursements

Year	**1**	**2**	**3**	**4**	**5**	**6**
Expense reimbursements	$31,454	$34,617	$37,888	$41,451	$44,845	$48,355

Rodale Law had negotiated a $4.25-per-square-foot expense stop; therefore, the landlord would be responsible for all operating expenses up to $4.25 per square foot. The tenant is required to reimburse the landlord for all operating expenses exceeding the $4.25-per-square-foot expense stop. Therefore, the expense reimbursements for the first year can be calculated using the following procedure:

1. The total operating expenses for the first year ($188,379) are divided by the building rentable area (30,000 square feet) to calculate the actual operating expenses per square foot for the subject property ($6.2793).
2. The expense stop of $4.25 is deducted from $6.279 to calculate the operating expenses per square foot that exceed the stop ($2.0293).
3. The result from Step 2 is then multiplied by the tenant's rentable square feet (15,500) to calculate the total expense reimbursement for the first year ($2.0293 × 15,500 = $31,454). This same process is repeated for subsequent years in the analysis.

H&B Accounting Contract

- Operating expense terms: Full service (gross lease)
- Reimbursements

Year	1	2	3	4	5	6
Expense reimbursements	0	0	0	0	0	0

A full-service or gross lease requires that the landlord pay for all operating expenses; as a result, no reimbursements are noted for H&B Accounting.

Suite D Contract

- Operating expense terms: $5.00 per square foot expense stop
- Reimbursements

Year	1	2	3	4	5	6
Expense reimbursements	$3,070	$3,560	$4,067	$4,618	$5,144	$5,687

The contract for Suite D provides for a dollar expense stop of $5.00 per square foot. The procedure for calculating the landlord reimbursement is similar to that provided previously for Rodale Law; therefore, the calculation will be a practice exercise. The total operating expense reimbursements are illustrated in Exhibit 5.9.

Once the operating expense reimbursements have been calculated, the total income can be calculated as shown in Exhibit 5.9. The appraiser in the Maple Landing case noted that investors in this market apply a 5% vacancy allowance to collected rental income, even when properties are fully occupied. Notice that, in this instance, the vacancy allowance is applied only to the rental income. One could argue that if the 5% vacancy were applied to the rental income, then

Exhibit 5.9 **Maple Landing Expense Reimbursement Forecast**

Year	1	2	3	4	5	6
Income						
Diamond Wednesday, Inc.	$87,750	$87,750	$87,750	$87,750	$87,750	$87,750
Rodale Law	$244,125	$249,008	$253,988	$259,067	$264,249	$269,534
H&B Accounting	$129,200	$133,722	$138,402	$152,000	$152,000	$152,000
Suite D	$38,400	$39,744	$41,135	$42,575	$44,065	$45,607
Potential rental income	$499,475	$510,224	$521,275	$541,392	$548,064	$554,891
Other income	0	0	0	0	0	0
Expense reimbursements						
Diamond Wednesday, Inc.	$28,257	$29,175	$30,125	$31,159	$32,144	$33,163
Rodale Law	$31,454	$34,617	$37,888	$41,451	$44,845	$48,355
H&B Accounting	0	0	0	0	0	0
Suite D	$3,070	$3,560	$4,067	$4,618	$5,144	$5,687
Total expense reimbursements	$62,781	$67,352	$72,079	$77,228	$82,133	$87,205
Total income	$562,256	$577,576	$593,354	$618,621	$630,197	$642,096
Vacancy allowance 5%	$24,974	$25,511	$26,064	$27,070	$27,403	$27,745
Effective gross income	$537,283	$552,065	$567,290	$591,551	$602,794	$614,352
Operating expenses						
Property taxes	$64,000	$66,560	$69,222	$71,991	$74,871	$77,866
Property insurance	$6,900	$7,107	$7,320	$7,540	$7,766	$7,999
Property management	$19,979	$20,409	$20,851	$21,656	$21,923	$22,196
Common area maintenance	$97,500	$100,425	$103,438	$106,541	$109,737	$113,029
Total operating expenses	$188,379	$194,501	$200,831	$207,728	$214,297	$221,090
Net operating income	$348,904	$357,564	$366,459	$383,823	$388,497	$393,262
Leasing commissions						
Tenant improvements						
Capital improvements						
Cash flow before debt service						

it should also be applied to the expense reimbursements. The Maple Landing Case Study does not require that the vacancy allowance also be applied to the operating expense reimbursements. In addition, the Argus software default is to apply general vacancy to the rental income and not to the expense reimbursements, and this convention is followed here. In practice, the appraiser should research the methodology used in the marketplace and be consistent in his or her application. Once the vacancy allowance is deducted, the effective gross income and net operating income can be calculated, as illustrated in the exhibit.

Estimating Leasing Expenditures and Capital Costs

Leasing expenditures generally include leasing commissions and tenant improvement allowances. Leasing commissions are earned by leasing agents when they find tenants that execute a lease and occupy space in an office building. Typically, leasing commissions are paid up front when the tenant occupies the rented space; however, in some situations the leasing agent may be paid over time with the lease payments. The appraiser should investigate this issue to determine what procedure is typical in the current market and carefully examine the potential leasing commission differential for a renewal tenant versus a new tenant. Typically, the owner pays a lower commission for renewal tenants than for new tenants.

Commercial office construction generally allows for multiple interior configurations (build-outs), depending on the tenant requirements. The build-out of the interior space is referred to as *tenant improvements*. The actual cost of tenant improvements is negotiable and frequently paid by both landlord and tenant. The landlord's contribution to the interior build-out is referred to as a *tenant improvement allowance*. Depending on market conditions, the landlord may be obligated to provide a tenant improvement allowance in order to entice prospective tenants to sign a lease and occupy the space.

Capital costs are expenditures that increase the value and/or the useful life of the property. In addition, they are typically nonrecurring, at least in an annual sense. An expenditure that maintains value is considered an operating expense. A replacement allowance (reserve) is an allowance that provides for the periodic replacement of building components that wear out more rapidly than the building itself and must be replaced during the building's economic life.

On a practical basis, reserves for replacements are future capital expenditures that are "smoothed" to accommodate the direct capitalization of a single year's income. The proper treatment of leasing expenses and capital costs requires clear identification of the valuation method used by the appraiser. For instance, if direct or mortgage-equity capitalization techniques are used, the appraiser may estimate net operating income without deducting leasing expenses or capital costs–as long as the appraiser is consistent with the comparable data and the subject property.[3] This also holds with the application of replacement allowances. For example, when using direct or mortgage-equity capitalization, the operating statement may be depicted as

Potential Gross Income
– Vacancy Loss
Effective Gross Income
– Operating Expenses
Net Operating Income

3. The appraiser must examine the methodologies used by market participants and replicate these in the appraisal; therefore, if market participants are deducting reserves for the replacement of short-lived items, the appraiser should as well.

Market value is estimated by capitalizing the net operating income by the capitalization rate. If, however, discounted cash flow analysis (yield capitalization) is employed, leasing expenses and capital costs are typically deducted after the net operating income to arrive at a cash flow before debt service or net cash flow. This approach is generally used by contemporary lease analysis software. In this instance, the operating statement is depicted as

	Potential Gross Income
–	Vacancy Loss
	Effective Gross Income
–	Operating Expenses
	Net Operating Income
–	Leasing and Capital Costs
	Cash Flow Before Debt Service

The cash flow before debt service is estimated for each period over the anticipated projection period. Market value is estimated by discounting the cash flow before debt service for each period and the reversion by an appropriate discount rate.

Maple Landing Case Study: Estimating Leasing Expenditures and Capital Costs

The following table summarizes the leasing and capital costs for the Maple Landing Case Study:

Year	1	2	3	4	5	6
Leasing commissions	$11,949			$15,200		
Tenant improvements	$28,800			$30,400		
Capital improvements				$40,000		

Leasing Commissions

The Maple Landing case states that leasing commissions will be paid up front, based on the rental revenue forecast for the respective tenants. Suite D is a new tenant that recently signed a lease. At the time of occupancy, which is in the first month of the analysis, the landlord will be obligated to pay a leasing commission of $11,949 to the leasing agent. This amounts to 4% of the total rental revenue ($298,729) estimated for Suite D over the term of the lease. Exhibit 5.10 illustrates the rental income for Suite D for the first six years; however, the term of the lease is seven years, so rental income for the seventh year must also be estimated.

H&B Accounting will renew their lease beginning in Year 4. The terms of the new lease call for a fixed rent of $20 per square foot for five years. This

Exhibit 5.10	Rental Income for Suite D						
Year	**1**	**2**	**3**	**4**	**5**	**6**	**7**
Income							
Suite D	$38,400	$39,744	$41,135	$42,575	$44,065	$45,607	$47,203

amounts to $152,000 per year, or $760,000 for the term of the lease. The renewal leasing commission is 2%, which amounts to a $15,200 leasing commission expenditure in Year 4.

Tenant Improvement Allowance

A tenant improvement allowance of $12 per square foot of rental area is provided for Suite D in Year 1. At 2,400 square feet of rentable area, this amounts to a $28,800 tenant improvement expenditure. H&B Accounting is provided a tenant improvement allowance of $4 per square foot of rental area to refresh their space at the time of renewal. At 7,600 square feet, this amounts to a tenant improvement allowance expenditure of $30,400 in Year 4.

Capital Expenditure

At the time of renovation, the owners elected to postpone the replacement of the roof; however, all parties agree that a capital expenditure of $40,000 to replace the roof will be required in about four years. Therefore, a capital expenditure of $40,000 is forecast in Year 4 of the analysis.

Section 6. Forecasting Cash Flows

Once rental revenue, vacancies, operating expenses, and leasing and capital costs have been estimated, the cash flows over the anticipated projection period can be forecast.

Maple Landing Case Study: Forecasting Cash Flows

Exhibit 5.11 shows the forecast cash flows for the Maple Landing office property.

Exhibit 5.11 Maple Landing Forecast Cash Flows

Year	1	2	3	4	5	6
Income						
Diamond Wednesday, Inc.	$87,750	$87,750	$87,750	$87,750	$87,750	$87,750
Rodale Law	$244,125	$249,008	$253,988	$259,067	$264,249	$269,534
H&B Accounting	$129,200	$133,722	$138,402	$152,000	$152,000	$152,000
Suite D	$38,400	$39,744	$41,135	$42,575	$44,065	$45,607
Potential rental income	$499,475	$510,224	$521,275	$541,392	$548,064	$554,891
Other income	0	0	0	0	0	0
Expense reimbursements						
Diamond Wednesday, Inc.	$28,257	$29,175	$30,125	$31,159	$32,144	$33,163
Rodale Law	$31,454	$34,617	$37,888	$41,451	$44,845	$48,355
H&B Accounting	0	0	0	0	0	0
Suite D	$3,070	$3,560	$4,067	$4,618	$5,144	$5,687
Total expense reimbursements	$62,781	$67,352	$72,079	$77,228	$82,133	$87,205
Total income	$562,256	$577,576	$593,354	$618,621	$630,197	$642,096
Vacancy allowance 5%	$24,974	$25,511	$26,064	$27,070	$27,403	$27,745
Effective gross income	$537,283	$552,065	$567,290	$591,551	$602,794	$614,352
Operating expenses						
Property taxes	$64,000	$66,560	$69,222	$71,991	$74,871	$77,866
Property insurance	$6,900	$7,107	$7,320	$7,540	$7,766	$7,999
Property management	$19,979	$20,409	$20,851	$21,656	$21,923	$22,196
Common area maintenance	$97,500	$100,425	$103,438	$106,541	$109,737	$113,029
Total operating expenses	$188,379	$194,501	$200,831	$207,728	$214,297	$221,090
Net operating income	$348,904	$357,564	$366,459	$383,823	$388,497	$393,262
Leasing commissions	$11,949			$15,200		
Tenant improvements	$28,800			$30,400		
Capital improvements				$40,000		
Cash flow before debt service	$308,154	$357,564	$366,459	$298,223	$388,497	

Note: Calculations may vary due to rounding.

Section 7. Direct Capitalization and Yield Capitalization

Income valuation models can be divided into two basic categories: ratio models (direct capitalization) and discounted cash flow models (yield capitalization). *Direct capitalization* is formally defined as "a method used to convert an estimate of a single year's income expectancy into an indication of value in one direct step, either by dividing the net income estimate by an appropriate capitalization rate or by multiplying the income estimate by an appropriate factor. Direct capitalization employs capitalization rates and multipliers extracted from market data. Only one year's income is used. Yield and value change are implied, but not identified."[4]

As noted in the definition, the income estimate can be divided by an appropriate rate or multiplied by an appropriate factor. The rate that is typically employed in this context is the overall capitalization rate or the mortgage-equity capitalization rate. The factor typically employed is the effective gross income multiplier. Both of these methodologies will be described in this section.

Overall Capitalization Rate

Direct capitalization from an overall rate requires a three-step process.

1. Estimate the net operating income (I_O) for the subject property and the comparables (be consistent in the calculation).
2. Calculate the overall capitalization rate (R_O) for each comparable by dividing the net operating income (I_O) by the sale price.
3. Select the appropriate capitalization rate (R_O) and capitalize the subject's net operating income (I_O) to provide an estimate of value.

Selecting an appropriate overall capitalization rate for the subject property from the comparable sales requires that the appraiser consider the compatibility of the property attributes, the transaction characteristics, and the risk characteristics. The appraiser must provide sound reasoning for the selection of the capitalization rate. In addition, the appraiser must be careful to not use measures of central tendency, such as an arithmetic mean, which can be heavily influenced by outliers.

For instance, assume that the appraiser has researched the comparable sales summarized in Exhibit 5.12. The capitalization rates range from 8.1% to 8.9%. Similar to the bracketing and narrowing process that will be discussed in the chapter on the sales comparison approach, the appraiser examines each of the transactions in an effort to determine an appropriate and market-supported capitalization rate for the subject property. This narrowing process results from considering the physical, locational, financial, and transactional characteristics of each property in comparison to the subject.

---

4. *The Appraisal of Real Estate*, 499.

Exhibit 5.12 Summary Grid of Comparable Sales

Comparable	Subject	1	2	3	4	5
Sale price		$3,870,000	$5,200,000	$3,850,000	$3,450,000	$3,200,000
Price per sq. ft. (gross)		$122.86	$144.44	$128.33	$107.81	$110.34
Price per sq. ft. (rentable)		$135.01	$148.91	$142.59	$114.69	$125.39
Price per sq. ft. (usable)		$148.51	$166.78	$154.00	$127.31	$145.45
NOI per sq. ft. (gross)		$9.95	$11.99	$10.91	$9.60	$9.60
NOI per sq. ft. (rentable)		$10.94	$12.36	$12.12	$10.21	$10.91
NOI per sq. ft. (usable)		$12.03	$13.84	$13.09	$11.33	$12.65
Property rights conveyed	Leased fee	Leased fee	Leased fee	Leased fee	Below mkt.	Leased fee
Financing terms	Market	Market	Market	Favorable	Market	Market
Conditions of sale	Normal	Normal	Normal	Normal	Normal	Normal
Exp. made after purchase	None	None	None	None	None	None
Date of sale (market conditions)	Current date	2 mos. ago	12 mos. ago	6 mos. ago	8 mos. ago	13 mos. ago
Location	Good	Similar	Similar	Superior	Similar	Inferior
Physical characteristics						
Site area (sq. ft.)	104,575	98,438	112,500	85,714	106,667	107,407
Site utility	Good	Similar	Similar	Similar	Inferior	Similar
Gross building area (sq. ft.)	32,000	31,500	36,000	30,000	32,000	29,000
Rentable building area (sq. ft.)	29,120	28,665	34,920	27,000	30,080	25,520
Usable building area (sq. ft.)	26,000	26,059	31,179	25,000	27,099	22,000
Age/condition	5 yrs./good	8 yrs./good	1 yr./excell.	3 yrs./good	22 yrs./avg.	4 yrs./good
Parking ratio (stalls per 1,000 sq. ft.)	1.7	1.9	3	1.2	3.1	2.7
Land-to-bldg. ratio	3.27	3.13	3.13	2.86	3.33	3.70
Floor area ratio	31%	32%	32%	35%	30%	27%
Bldg. load factor	12%	10%	12%	8%	11%	16%
Efficiency ratio	91%	91%	97%	90%	94%	88%
Economic characteristics						
Overall capitalization rate		8.10%	8.30%	8.50%	8.90%	8.70%
Effective gross inc. multiplier		7.30	7.67	7.55	6.80	7.20

For the case study, an 8.5% capitalization rate was found to be supported; therefore, property value is estimated as follows:

$$\frac{NOI}{R_O} = \text{Value } \frac{\$348{,}904}{0.085} = \$4{,}104{,}753\text{, rounded to } \$4{,}100{,}000$$

Mortgage-Equity Capitalization Rate

Direct capitalization from mortgage-equity analysis recognizes that when debt is used, the lender and equity investor are due a return *on* and *of* the investment. The *mortgage-equity technique*, sometimes referred to as the *band-of-investment technique*, derives a capitalization rate by calculating the weighted average of the first-year cash returns to the lender and the equity investor. The formula for mortgage-equity analysis is

$$R_O = M \times R_M + (1 - M) \times R_E$$

Where

M = loan-to-value ratio

R_M = mortgage constant

$(1 - M)$ = equity proportion

R_E = equity dividend rate

This technique assumes that similar properties are being acquired with debt and equity–i.e., a mortgage loan from a financial institution (debt) and a down payment (equity) from the equity investor. The mortgage loan requires that the owner make a monthly payment. When the monthly payment is annualized, this summation is referred to as an *annual debt service* (DS). Deducting the debt service from the net operating income (I_O) results in a before-tax cash flow (BTCF). Therefore, the net operating income can be thought of as being distributed to the holders of the debt and the equity. This is illustrated as follows:

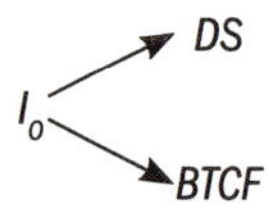

In direct capitalization, $R_O = I_O / P$, where P = purchase price ≈ (approximately equals) value. Because net operating income can be partitioned between debt service (DS) and before-tax cash flow (BTCF), the debt service can be considered the net income to the mortgage or the debt and the before-tax cash flow can be considered the net income to the equity. Therefore, the following equalities result:

$$R_M = \frac{DS}{LoanAmt} \qquad R_E = \frac{BTCF}{EquityAmt} \qquad R_O = \frac{I_O}{P}$$

R_M is the mortgage capitalization rate and R_E is the equity capitalization rate (also referred to as the *equity dividend rate* or the *before-tax, cash-on-cash return*). The purchase price (P) can be derived by combining the loan amount and the equity amount. As a result, the capitalization rate (R_O) can be thought of as the weighted average of the mortgage capitalization rate (R_M) and the equity capitalization rate (R_E). Once R_O is derived, the subject's value can be estimated by dividing the subject property's net operating income (I_O) by the capitalization rate (R_O). It is important to know that the mortgage capitalization rate (R_M) can be derived two ways:

1. Annual debt service can be divided by the loan amount, as illustrated previously.

2. The mortgage constant can be calculated, if the terms of the mortgage (interest rate, payment frequency, and loan term) are known.

The derivation of the latter technique is shown in the following equation:

$$PVA = Ann\left[\frac{1-\frac{1}{(1+\frac{i}{m})^{n*m}}}{\frac{i}{m}}\right] \quad (1)$$

Where

PVA = Present value of an annuity
Ann = Periodic annuity payment
i = Annual mortgage interest rate
n = Term of the mortgage in years
m = Frequency of payments per year

The term in brackets is referred to as the present value annuity factor. Note that the loan amount and debt service can be substituted for *PVA* and $Ann \times m$, as shown in the following equation:

$$LoanAmt = DS\left[\frac{1-\frac{1}{(1+\frac{i}{m})^{n*m}}}{\frac{i}{m}}\right] \quad (2)$$

The reciprocal of the present value annuity factor is the mortgage constant.

$$\frac{DS}{LoanAmt} = \frac{\frac{i}{m}}{1-\frac{1}{\left(1+\frac{i}{m}\right)^{n*m}}} \times m = R_M = MC \quad (3)$$

Mortgage-Equity (Band-of-Investment) Practice Problem

After researching market data and talking with market participants, the appraiser finds that before-tax, cash-on-cash returns (equity dividend rates) cluster around 6% and typical loan terms are as follows:

Loan Information	
Loan-to-value ratio	75%
Mortgage interest rate	8.0%
Loan amortization period	20 years
Periodic payments per year	12

Based on this information, determine the overall capitalization rate using the band-of-investment technique and compute the value of the case study subject property.

Solution

$$R_O = M \times R_M + (1 - M) \times R_E$$

$$R_O = 0.75 \times \left[\frac{\frac{0.080}{12}}{1 - \frac{1}{\left(1 + \frac{0.080}{12}\right)^{20 \times 12}}} \times 12 \right] + 0.25 \times 0.06$$

$$0.75 \times 0.100373 + 0.25 \times 0.060 = 0.0903$$

Then

$$\frac{NOI}{R_O} = \text{Value} \; \frac{\$348{,}904}{0.0903} = \$3{,}863{,}832, \text{ rounded to } \$3{,}900{,}000$$

Underwriter's Method

Deriving a capitalization rate from an underwriter's method requires use of the following equation:

$$R_O = DCR \times R_M \times M$$

Where

R_O = the overall capitalization rate

DCR = the typical debt coverage ratio $\frac{I_O}{DS}$

R_M = the typical mortgage constant or mortgage capitalization rate

M = the typical loan-to-value ratio

Care must be taken when using the underwriter's method because it only considers the perspective of the lender rather than that of both the lender and equity investor. To ensure that the result is market-based, the inputs should come from comparable sales and market surveys rather than directly from a single lender. This ensures that the capitalization rate will be market based. Application of this capitalization rate to the subject property's net operating income results in a market value estimate.

For example, assume that a survey of market participants and mortgage lenders finds that a debt coverage ratio of 1.15 is typical in the market. Also, assume that a mortgage constant and loan-to-value ratio of 10% and 75%, respectively, are typical in this market. (Note that these estimates are the same as those inputs used in the band-of-investment technique.) Therefore, the capitalization rate is calculated as

$$\begin{aligned} R_O &= DCR \times R_M \times M \\ &= 1.15 \times 0.10 \times 0.75 \\ &= 0.08625 \end{aligned}$$

Applying this capitalization rate to the Maple Landing office property results in the following value estimate:

$$\frac{NOI}{R_0} = \frac{\$348{,}904}{0.08625} = \$4{,}045{,}264, \text{ rounded to } \$4{,}000{,}000$$

Effective Gross Income Multiplier

The effective gross income multiplier (*EGIM*) is defined as the ratio between the sale price (or value) of a property and its effective gross income, or as a single year's *EGI* expectancy or annual average of several years' *EGI* expectancies (*EGIM* = *V*/*EGI*).

The application of the effective gross income multiplier is very straightforward. First, effective gross income multipliers are derived from the comparable sales. Second, an appropriate effective gross income multiplier is selected and applied to the subject property's effective gross income to result in an estimate of value (*EGIM* × *EGI* = *V*). Without being redundant, the bracketing and narrowing process is very similar to the process discussed in the direct capitalization approach. For the Maple Landing Case Study property, the first-year effective gross income was estimated at $537,283. The comparables shown in Exhibit 5.12 show a range in effective gross income multipliers of 6.8 to 7.67. Assuming that a multiplier of 7.5 is considered reasonable for the subject property, a value estimate of $4,029,623 would be calculated.

$$EGIM \times EGI = Value$$

$$7.5 \times \$537{,}283 = \$4{,}029{,}623, \text{ rounded to } \$4{,}000{,}000$$

Yield Capitalization

Yield capitalization is the method used to convert future benefits into present value by discounting each future benefit at an appropriate yield rate or developing an overall rate that explicitly reflects the investment's income pattern, value change, and yield rate.

Prior to the advent of the computer, income models such as *J*-factor and *K*-factor analyses, which assumed constant rates of growth, were frequently used to account for changes in income over the anticipated projection period. However, these models are used less frequently today because computer software allows the appraiser to model the anticipated future income directly. The contemporary method is preferred because the constant growth rate assumptions required in the historical techniques may not reflect reality. In other words, future income may not grow at a constant rate because differing lease terms in an office property typically do not grow at constant rates. This contemporary method is referred to as *discounted cash flow analysis* and is accomplished in three basic steps.

1. The appraiser estimates the cash flows before debt service over the estimated projection period.
2. The appraiser estimates the property reversion at the end of the projection period.

3. The appraiser discounts the cash flow before debt service and the property reversion to the present period at an appropriate discount rate.

The property reversion is synonymous with the forecast future value of the property at the end of the projection period, less selling expenses. The forecast future value of the property is calculated by capitalizing the net operating income in period $n + 1$, where n is the projection period calculated by a *reversionary capitalization rate*, sometimes referred to as a *going-out capitalization rate* or a *terminal capitalization rate*. The reversionary capitalization rate is the rate applied to the expected ultimate sale price or value of a building after a multi-year holding period; it is typically about 50 basis points higher than a going-in capitalization rate.

A survey of market participants generally provides the best estimate of a reversionary capitalization rate. It was noted in the Maple Landing Case Study that the reversionary capitalization rates were 25 basis points higher than direct or going-in capitalization rates, which results in a reversionary capitalization rate of 8.75% for the Maple Landing property. After estimating the future value of the property at the end of the projection period, the reversion is calculated by deducting selling expenses as follows:

Future Sale Price
– Selling Expenses
Reversion

Maple Landing Case Study: Reversion Calculation

$$\frac{\text{6th Year } NOI}{\text{Reversionary Cap Rate}} = \text{Future Sale Price}$$

$$\frac{\$393{,}262}{0.0875} = \$4{,}494{,}423$$

Future Sale Price		$4,494,423	
– Selling Expenses	=	– 224,721	(5%)
Reversion		$4,269,702	

Adding the reversion to the cash flows before debt service results in the following forecast cash flows:

Year	1	2	3	4	5
Cash flows before debt service	$308,154	$357,564	$366,459	$298,223	$388,497
Reversion					$4,269,702
Total	$308,154	$357,564	$366,459	$298,223	$4,658,199

ount Rate

en timated over the holding period, calculated by discounting them ing the discount rate is the free and n required by the typical inves- d r of return for an investment by aring returns available on alter- opp tunities. Investors may build up nents of compensation.

fre rate)

t

sk

es rs building up a discount rate:

	3%
	1%
	2%
	3%
	9%

chnique to formulate an appro- ou generally be inappropriate for rt rates used by market partici- our rates. To estimate an appropriate praisers must carefully survey an selling similar properties in the es, discount rates tend to cluster ila ocations. In the survey process, nmunicate with the market par- par g apples to apples." For instance, ee and clear, before-tax rate of cash flows before debt service.

After researching and surveying the primary market, it is often helpful to benchmark the results with third-party data. An example of third-party data is provided in Exhibit 5.13.

Once the discount rate is selected, the forecast cash flows are discounted to the present by multiplying the cash flows by the present value factors. A present value factor is calculated as

$$PV = \frac{1}{(1+i)^n}$$

Where

PV = present value	i = discount rate
FV = future value	n = term (years)

Exhibit 5.13 Korpacz Real Estate Investor Survey: Dallas Office Market, Third Quarter 2006

Key Indicators	Current Quarter	Last Quarter	Year Ago
Discount Rate (*IRR*)[a]			
Range	7.50% - 11.50%	7.50% - 11.50%	8.00% - 11.50%
Average	9.13%	9.13%	9.53%
Change (basis points)	–	0	-40
Overall Cap Rate (*OAR*)[a]			
Range	6.00% - 10.00%	6.00% - 10.00%	7.00% - 10.00%
Average	8.21%	8.33%	8.65%
Change (basis points)	–	-12	-44
Residual Cap Rate			
Range	7.00%-11.00%	7.00%-11.00%	7.25%-11.00%
Average	8.69%	8.75%	9.00%
Change (basis points)	–	06	031
Market Rent Change Rate[b]			
Range	0.00%-5.00%	0.00%-4.00%	0.00%-3.00%
Average	2.80%	2.31%	1.50%
Change (basis points)	–	+49	+130
Expense Change Rate[b]			
Range	2.00%-3.00%	2.00%-3.00%	2.00%-3.00%
Average	2.67%	2.80%	2.80%
Change (basis points)	–	-13	-13
Average Marketing Time			
Range	3.00-12.00	3.00-12.00	3.00-12.00
Average	6.30	6.38	6.38
Change (basis points)	–	-1.25	-1.25

a. Rate on unleveraged, all-cash transactions

b. Initial rate of change

Source: PricewaterhouseCoopers. Used with permission.

Maple Landing Case Study: Selecting an Appropriate Discount Rate

For the Maple Landing Case Study, investors are using an approximate 10% discount rate when discounting the cash flows before debt service and the reversion to arrive at a value estimate.

Exhibit 5.14 illustrates the calculation of the present values for each period by multiplying the cash flow before debt service by the present value factors. The summation of the present value calculations results in the total present value of the subject property.

Based on the calculations shown in Exhibit 5.14, the estimated market value of the Maple Landing office/retail property via the discounted cash flow analysis is $3,947,038, rounded to $3,950,000. Exhibits 5.15 and 5.16 are summaries of the operating statement and the present value of the forecast cash flows for the Maple Landing property as generated by Argus Valuation–DCF software. Notice that the valuation results are identical to those generated by hand.

Exhibit 5.14 DCF Analysis for the Maple Landing Case Study

Period	Cash Flow Before Debt Service	Present Value Factors	Present Value
1	$308,154	0.9090900	$280,140
2	$357,564	0.8264463	295,507
3	$366,459	0.7513148	275,326
4	$298,223	0.6830135	203,690
5	$388,497	0.6209213	241,226
Reversion	$4,269,701	0.6209213	2,651,149
Total present value			$3,947,038

Exhibit 5.15 Operating Statement (Maple Landing Office/Retail Property) Generated by Argus Software

Software: ARGUS Ver. 12.0.4 (Build: 12000-G)
File: Maple Landing
Property Type: Office & Retail
Portfolio:

Date: 1/31/07
Time: 12:49 pm
Ref#: AGI
Page: 1

Schedule Of Prospective Cash Flow
In Inflated Dollars for the Fiscal Year Beginning 1/1/2006

For the Years Ending	Year 1 Dec-2006	Year 2 Dec-2007	Year 3 Dec-2008	Year 4 Dec-2009	Year 5 Dec-2010	Year 6 Dec-2011
Potential Gross Revenue						
Base Rental Revenue	$499,475	$510,224	$521,275	$541,392	$548,064	$554,891
Scheduled Base Rental Revenue	499,475	510,224	521,275	541,392	548,064	554,891
Expense Reimbursement Revenue						
Property Taxes	21,329	23,048	24,844	26,765	28,696	30,713
Property Insurance	2,299	2,461	2,627	2,804	2,976	3,155
Management	6,659	7,067	7,484	8,050	8,402	8,754
CAM	32,494	34,776	37,124	39,610	42,059	44,582
Total Reimbursement Revenue	62,781	67,352	72,079	77,229	82,133	87,204
Total Potential Gross Revenue	562,256	577,576	593,354	618,621	630,197	642,095
General Vacancy	(24,974)	(25,511)	(26,064)	(27,070)	(27,403)	(27,745)
Effective Gross Revenue	537,282	552,065	567,290	591,551	602,794	614,350
Operating Expenses						
Property Taxes	64,000	66,560	69,222	71,991	74,871	77,866
Property Insurance	6,900	7,107	7,320	7,540	7,766	7,999
Management	19,979	20,409	20,851	21,656	21,923	22,196
CAM	97,500	100,425	103,438	106,541	109,737	113,029
Total Operating Expenses	188,379	194,501	200,831	207,728	214,297	221,090
Net Operating Income	348,903	357,564	366,459	383,823	388,497	393,260
Leasing & Capital Costs						
Tenant Improvements	28,800			30,400		
Leasing Commissions	11,885			15,200		
Roof Replacement				40,000		
Total Leasing & Capital Costs	40,685			85,600		
Cash Flow Before Debt Service & Taxes	$308,218	$357,564	$366,459	$298,223	$388,497	$393,260

Source: Argus Software. Used with permission

Exhibit 5.16 **Present Value Calculations (Maple Landing Office/Retail Property) Generated by Argus Software**

Software: ARGUS Ver. 12.0.4 (Build: 12000-G)	Date: 1/31/07
File: Maple Landing	Time: 12:49 pm
Property Type: Office & Retail	Ref#: AGI
Portfolio:	Page: 2

Prospective Present Value
Cash Flow Before Debt Service plus Property Resale
Discounted Annually (Endpoint on Cash Flow & Resale) over a 5-Year Period

Analysis Period	For the Year Ending	Annual Cash Flow	P.V. of Cash Flow @ 10.00%
Year 1	Dec-2006	$308,218	$280,198
Year 2	Dec-2007	357,564	295,508
Year 3	Dec-2008	366,459	275,326
Year 4	Dec-2009	298,223	203,690
Year 5	Dec-2010	388,497	241,226
Total Cash Flow		1,718,961	1,295,948
Property Resale @ 8.75% Cap		4,269,680	2,651,135
Total Property Present Value			$3,947,083
Rounded to Thousands			$3,947,000
Per SqFt			131.57

Percentage Value Distribution

Assured Income	33.38%
Prospective Income	-0.55%
Prospective Property Resale	67.17%
	100.00%

Source: Argus Software. Used with permission

Section 8. Reconciliation of the Income Capitalization Approach

Reconciliation is basically the process of evaluating the respective value conclusions derived from the different methodologies. This process essentially requires a reexamination of specific data, procedures, and techniques used to derive the alternative value estimates. Each valuation method or approach is reviewed and compared to the other approaches in terms of adequacy and reliability of data, soundness of analysis, and weight placed by market participants. It is imperative that the appraiser carefully consider and appropriately weight methodologies used most frequently by market participants as he or she concludes to a final opinion of value.

Maple Landing Case Study: Reconciliation of the Income Capitalization Approach

In terms of the Maple Landing Case Study, the alternative income capitalization techniques provide the following value estimates:

Direct capitalization	$4,100,000
Mortgage-equity capitalization	$3,900,000
Underwriter's method	$4,000,000
Effective gross income multiplier	$4,000,000
Discounted cash flow analysis	$3,950,000

At this stage, the appraiser would outline in the report the strengths and weaknesses of each of the income capitalization techniques. This would include a careful examination of the reliability of the data used in each valuation technique and the methodology used most frequently by market participants. In this case, the range is narrow enough that the appraiser would probably conclude to a value estimate of $4,000,000, unless there were substantial reasons to support an alternative lower or higher estimate, such as $3.9 to $4.1 million.

Section 9. Alternative Valuation Scenarios

Sections 1 through 8 of this chapter outlined the valuation methodology for estimating the market value of a multitenant office building with varying lease structures. In this case, the property rights appraised consisted of the leased fee interest, the property status was "as is," and the occupancy status was stabilized.

As noted at the beginning of this chapter, the property interest appraised, property status, and occupancy status may take many forms, depending on the scope of the appraisal (see Exhibit 5.17). These various combinations result in numerous potential valuation scenarios. It is essential that the appraiser clearly communicate with the client to determine the scope of the appraisal and then clearly articulate the valuation scenario in the appraisal report. The base valuation scenario described in previous sections assumed valuation of the property "as is" at stabilized occupancy, but other valuation scenarios are common.

Exhibit 5.17 illustrates the alternative valuation scenarios that may result from the various combinations of property rights appraised, property status, and occupancy status.

Exhibit 5.17 Alternative Valuation Scenarios

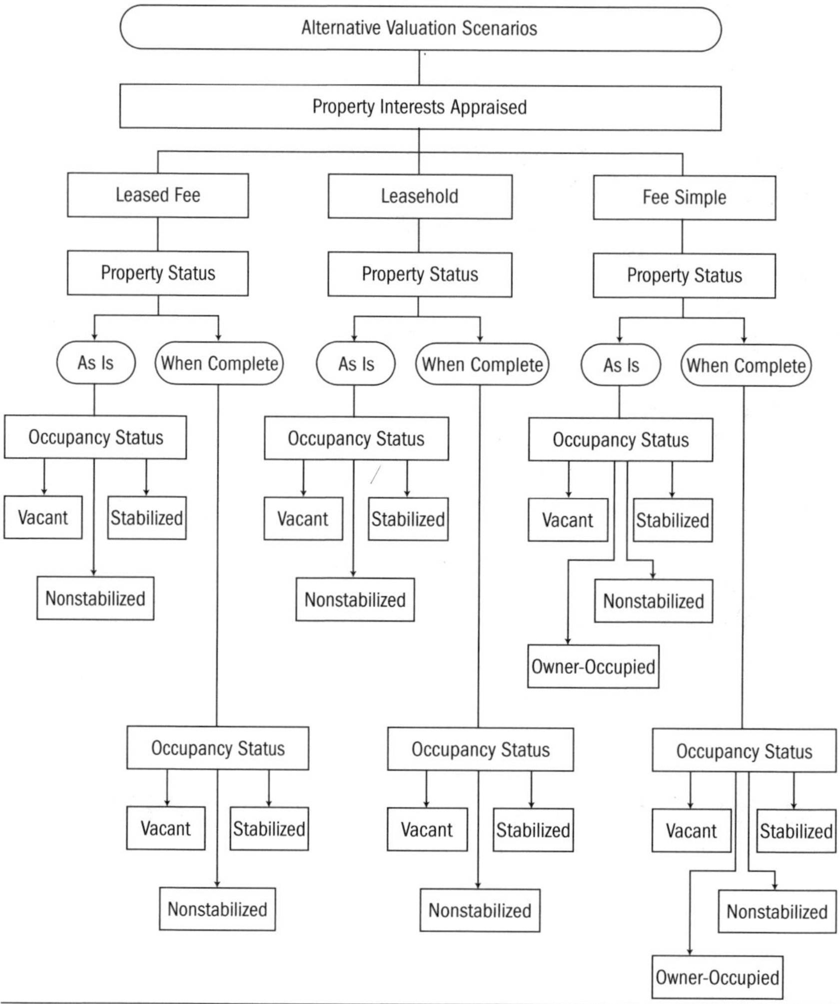

Although a review of all possible valuation scenarios is beyond the scope of this book, a review of two additional valuation scenarios is warranted. These two additional valuation scenarios are believed to be more commonly encountered by the appraiser and presented here as Valuation Scenarios 2 and 3.

Valuation Scenario 2

In Valuation Scenario 2, the property interest appraised is the fee-simple estate, the property status is "as is," and the property occupancy is stabilized. This valuation scenario requires that the appraiser use market rents, lease structures, operating expenses, capitalization rates, and yield rates.

Maple Landing Case Study: Valuation Scenario 2

Assume that market rents for the retail portion of the Maple Landing office property are $20 per square foot on an absolute net basis and that rents are forecast to increase at 3% per year. Also assume that market rents for the remaining office space are $16 per square foot on a full-service basis with a $4.50-per-sq.-ft. expense stop. Rents for the office space are expected to increase at 3% per year. Market participants allocate about 2% of effective gross income to cover leasing commissions and tenant improvements for a stabilized property. For the purposes of this analysis, assume that future capital expenditures amount to $40,000 for a new roof in Year 4, going-in capitalization rates are 8.5%, going-out capitalization rates are 8.75%, a five-year projection period is typically used, and a 5% stabilized vacancy is applied to rental income. Based on the revised cash flow statement, the "as is" market value of the fee-simple interest in the property at stabilized occupancy can be estimated as shown in Exhibit 5.18.

Capitalizing the first year's net operating income at 8.5% provides a value estimate of $4,215,882. Discounting the cash flow before debt service and reversion at 10% provides a value estimate of $4,315,227. Overall, this analysis finds that the "as is" market value of the fee simple interest in the property at stabilized occupancy ranges from $4.2 to $4.3 million.

Exhibit 5.18 Maple Landing Office/Retail Building Forecast Cash Flows

Year	1	2	3	4	5	6
Income						
Retail space (4,500 sq. ft. rentable)	$90,000	$92,700	$95,481	$98,345	$101,296	$104,335
Office space (25,500 sq. ft. rentable)	$408,000	$420,240	$432,847	$445,833	$459,208	$472,984
Potential rental income	$498,000	$512,940	$528,328	$544,178	$560,503	$577,318
Other income	0	0	0	0	0	0
Expense reimbursements						
Retail space (4,500 sq. ft. rentable)	$28,248	$29,191	$30,167	$31,176	$32,219	$33,298
Office space (25,500 sq. ft. rentable)	$45,322	$50,668	$56,196	$61,913	$67,825	$73,939
Total expense reimbursements	$73,570	$79,860	$86,363	$93,089	$100,044	$107,237
Total income	$571,570	$592,800	$614,692	$637,267	$660,548	$684,555
Vacancy allowance 5%	$24,900	$25,647	$26,416	$27,209	$28,025	$28,866
Effective gross income	$546,670	$567,153	$588,275	$610,058	$632,522	$655,689
Operating expenses						
Property taxes	$64,000	$66,560	$69,222	$71,991	$74,871	$77,866
Property insurance	$6,900	$7,107	$7,320	$7,540	$7,766	$7,999
Property management	$19,920	$20,518	$21,133	$21,767	$22,420	$23,093
Common area maintenance	$97,500	$100,425	$103,438	$106,541	$109,737	$113,029
Total operating expenses	$188,320	$194,610	$201,113	$207,839	$214,794	$221,987
Net operating income	$358,350	$372,543	$387,162	$402,219	$417,728	$433,703
Leasing commissions and TIs	$9,960	$10,259	$10,567	$10,884	$11,210	$11,546
Capital improvements				$40,000		
Cash flow before debt service	$348,390	$362,284	$376,595	$351,336	$406,518	

Note: Calculations may vary due to rounding.

Valuation Scenario 3

In Valuation Scenario 3, the property interest appraised is fee simple, the property status is "as is" and "when complete," and the occupancy status is vacant and stabilized. This scenario results in three separate values and is frequently requested by clients when properties are proposed or under construction. Mortgage lenders find the three separate values helpful in the underwriting process.

First, the lender wants an "as is" market value estimate of the fee simple interest to establish a collateral value at the onset of the loan, even though the proposed improvements have not been constructed or are not complete. The "as is" value in this case is typically land value. Methods for estimating land value are presented in the cost approach in Chapter 7. If the property has building improvements that do not contribute to value, then demolition costs will have to be considered and deducted to estimate the "as is" value. Even if the proposed improvements are under construction at the date of valuation, the lender will typically request that the appraiser do a land valuation rather than attempt to estimate the value of a partially completed structure.

After estimating land value, the next step is to estimate the market value of the fee simple interest in the property when complete. A property is usually not occupied at the completion of construction; therefore, the value estimate must account for the future absorption of the vacant space until it reaches stabilized occupancy. Once the future absorption and market rental rates are estimated, the future cash flows can be discounted to the present to estimate market value.

Maple Landing Case Study: Valuation Scenario 3

Assume that the Maple Landing office building is proposed and market rents are forecast in the following table:

Year	1	2	3	4	5	6	7	8
Retail space—rent per sq. ft. (net lease)	$20	$21	$22	$23	$24	$25	$26	$27
Office space—rent per sq. ft. (full service)	$16	$17	$18	$19	$20	$21	$22	$23
Expense stop	$4.50	$4.75	$5.00	$5.25	$5.50	$5.75	$6.00	$6.25

Also assume that market analysis finds that the property will absorb the first floor retail and office space during the first year and will absorb the remaining office space, located on the second and third floors, during the next two years (10,000 square feet per year). Leases will be for a term of five years and tenant improvement and leasing commissions will be $12 per square foot and 4%, respectively. Applying these assumptions to the Maple Landing Case Study results in the cash flow statement shown in Exhibit 5.19.

Capitalizing the sixth year *NOI* by 8.75% and then deducting 5% selling expenses results in a reversion of $5,091,729. Discounting the cash flows before debt service and the reversion at 10% results in a market value estimate when complete of $4,127,311, rounded to $4.1 million. The stabilized value can be estimated by capitalizing the stabilized *NOI* in Year 4 by a market capitalization rate, which has been shown previously.

Exhibit 5.19 Maple Landing Office/Retail Building Forecast Cash Flows

Year	1	2	3	4	5	6
Total rentable square feet	30,000	30,000	30,000	30,000	30,000	30,000
Occupied square feet	10,000	20,000	30,000	30,000	30,000	30,000
Vacant square feet	20,000	10,000	0	0	0	0
Income						
Retail space (4,500 sq. ft. rentable)	$90,000	$94,500	$99,000	$103,500	$108,000	$112,500
Office space (25,500 sq. ft. rentable)	$88,000	$263,500	$459,000	$484,500	$510,000	$535,500
Potential rental income	$178,000	$358,000	$558,000	$558,000	$618,000	$648,000
Other income	0	0	0	0	0	0
Expense reimbursements						
Retail space (4,500 sq. ft. rentable)	$26,328	$28,262	$30,345	$31,439	$32,564	$33,722
Office space (25,500 sq. ft. rentable)	$7,429	$23,721	$44,455	$44,278	$44,280	$44,467
Total expense reimbursements	$33,757	$51,983	$74,800	$75,717	$76,844	$78,189
Total income	$211,757	$409,983	$632,800	$663,717	$694,844	$726,189
Vacancy allowance 5%	$8,900	$17,900	$27,900	$29,400	$30,900	$32,400
Effective gross income	$202,857	$392,083	$604,900	$634,317	$663,944	$693,789
Operating expenses						
Property taxes	$64,000	$66,560	$69,222	$71,991	$74,871	$77,866
Property insurance	$6,900	$7,107	$7,320	$7,540	$7,766	$7,999
Property management	$7,120	$14,320	$22,320	$23,520	$24,720	$25,920
Common area maintenance	$97,500	$100,425	$103,438	$106,541	$109,737	$113,029
Total operating expenses	$175,520	$188,412	$202,300	$209,592	$217,094	$224,814
Net operating income	$27,337	$203,671	$402,600	$424,725	$446,850	$468,975
Leasing commissions	$39,600	$38,000	$40,000			
Tenant improvements	$120,000	$120,000	$120,000			
Capital improvements						
Cash flow before debt service	($12,263)	$165,671	$362,600	$424,725	$446,850	

Chapter 6

The Sales Comparison Approach

Of the three approaches to value, the sales comparison approach is by far the most intuitive. In its simplest form, this approach can be considered to be the "prudent shopper's approach." A prudent shopper carefully examines the item that he or she is interested in and then begins the comparison process by examining prices of similar items. Any differences in the items are considered, and adjustments to the respective prices are made to assist the shopper in selecting the "best deal." In effect, the prudent shopper exposes any arbitrage opportunities that result in an inefficient market.

Appraisers using the sales comparison approach effectively simulate the prudent shopper's experience to arrive at an estimate of value. Appraisers first familiarize themselves with the characteristics of the subject property and then research the market for similar properties that have recently sold, are listed for sale, or are under contract. They then compare these properties and transactions to the subject property, adjusting for necessary differences, to arrive at an estimate of value for the subject. The basic theoretical premise behind the sales comparison approach is the principle of substitution–i.e., it would not be rational for a buyer to pay more for a property than what he or she would pay for an equally desirable substitute.

The availability of substitute or comparable properties determines the applicability and reliability of the sales comparison approach. This approach is given considerable weight when numerous transactions for similar properties that have recently been sold are available. Conversely, this approach is given less weight when there are few properties that have transacted or are offered for sale or when there are significant differences between the subject property and the recently completed transactions. The latter case may result in large adjustments that may be difficult to support from market data.

The number of office property transactions available to appraisers differs by geographic area and market conditions. In a large metropolitan area that is experiencing considerable growth, transactions of office properties may be plentiful; however, in smaller markets that are experiencing economic declines, transactions of office properties may be scarce. The proportion of office properties compared to other commercial properties depends on the overall economic base of the geographic area.

Implementing the sales comparison approach requires that the appraiser follow a seven-step process.

Step 1. Identify subject property attributes
Step 2. Research comparable sales, listings, and contracts
Step 3. Confirm the comparable data with related parties
Step 4. Organize the data and calculate units of comparison
Step 5. Identify value-influencing differences between the subject property and the comparables (units of comparison)
Step 6. Adjust for these value-influencing differences
Step 7. Reconcile the analysis to arrive at an estimate of market value

Each of these steps is explained in detail in the following discussion.

Step 1. Identify Subject Property Attributes

Prior to researching comparable sales, the appraiser must familiarize him or herself with the characteristics and attributes of the subject property. This is typically done during the subject property inspection. The site and improvement analyses summarize the important physical and geographic aspects of the property. It is important that the appraiser carefully think about and identify the significant value-influencing characteristics during this process. Sometimes appraisers get distracted with "filling in the blanks" of a form and do not carefully reflect upon and examine the characteristics that have the greatest influence on value. Once this first step has been accomplished and the appraiser knows what to look for, he or she can then "go shopping," or begin to research comparable sales data.

Step 2. Research Comparable Sales, Listings, and Contracts

The primary objective of researching comparable sales is to identify recent transactions, listings, or properties under contract that are "most comparable" to the subject property and that would provide the best indication of value with the least amount of adjustment. Generally, location and property characteristics provide the basis for this search. The search process takes on a local perspective because data sources differ geographically. Potential sources of sales data include the county recorder's office, the county assessor's office, the local multiple listing service, third-party subscription services, real estate periodicals, and contacts with attorneys, brokers, lenders, and other appraisers.

In this search, it is essential that the appraiser carefully investigate and report the details of the subject property's sale history. The Uniform Standards of Professional Appraisal Practice (USPAP) require that

> When the value opinion to be developed is market value, an appraiser must, if such information is available to the appraiser in the normal course of business:
>
> (a) Analyze all agreements of sale, options, and listings of the subject property current as of the effective date of the appraisal; and
>
> (b) Analyze all sales of the subject property that occurred within the three (3) years prior to the effective date of the appraisal.[1]

Because location is a dominant value-influencing characteristic, the appraiser generally begins searching comparable data near the subject property and expands outward as needed. The search process stops once the appraiser has obtained sufficient comparable data to render a reliable estimate of value or until it is evident that comparable data is unavailable. Because of the small amount of commercial office transactions as compared to residential transactions, the process of finding an adequate number of comparable sales may require a significant time commitment and should not be underestimated by the novice appraiser.

Step 3. Confirm Comparable Data

Once the appraiser has identified prospective comparables, he or she must confirm the details of the transactions with knowledgeable parties and reliable sources. The comparables' physical characteristics–for example, building age and square footage–can be confirmed with on-site inspections and public records, such as assessor or city records. The transaction details can be confirmed with the buyer, seller, or broker. In states that require public disclosure of transaction prices, the appraiser can verify the data in the public record and inquire about possible anomalies, such as arm's-length nature and unusual financing terms. In non-disclosure states, the appraiser must attempt to finesse the transaction price data from the market participants. In this situation, the appraiser must attempt to verify the details with multiple sources to ensure the reliability of the data. In both cases, the appraiser must be careful to not violate public trust by disclosing confidential data.

Preparation is the key to successfully confirming comparable sales data. It is imperative that the appraiser carefully investigate all publicly available sources to obtain relevant data prior to actually contacting the buyer, seller, or broker in the transaction. If it is clear that the appraiser has done his or her "homework" and is familiar with the property and all publicly available data, the parties to the transaction are much more likely to assist the appraiser in confirming the more intimate details of the transaction. A comparable sale form can be helpful in organizing

---

1. Taken from Standards Rule 1-5 of USPAP, 2008-2009 edition. *Uniform Standards of Professional Appraisal Practice* (Washington, D.C.: The Appraisal Foundation, 2008), p. U-19. For further clarification, see USPAP Advisory Opinion 1, Sales History.

the data and documenting the property and transaction details. Exhibit 6.1 provides an example of a comparable sale form used in the valuation of office properties.

Exhibit 6.1 **Improved Comparable Sale Form**

Improved comparable no. ______________________________ Page 1

Property Identification Data

Property type: ______________________________

Address: ______________________________

Tax parcel number: ______________________________

Legal description (short): ______________________________

Sale Data

Sale price: ______________________________

Financing terms: ______________________________

Cash-equivalent sale price: ______________________________

Date of sale: ______________________________

Date of recordation: ______________________________

Instrument type: ______________________________

Grantor: ______________________________

Grantee: ______________________________

Marketing period: ______________________________

Confirmed with: ______________________________

Confirmed by: ______________________________

Confirmation date: ______________________________

Site Data

Shape/dimensions: ______________________________

Area: ______________________________

Zoning: ______________________________

Traffic count: ______________________________

Frontage: ______________________________

Legal access: ______________________________

Visibility: ______________________________

Topography: ______________________________

Utilities: ______________________________

Off-site improvements: ______________________________

Site utility: ______________________________

Exhibit 6.1 Improved Comparable Sale Form *(continued)*

Improvement Data Page 2

Building area: ____________________

Gross: ____________________

Rentable: ____________________

Usable: ____________________

Year built: ____________________

Age: ____________________

Condition: ____________________

Parking: ____________________

Elevators: ____________________

Floor area ratio (FAR): ____________________

Land-to-building ratio: ____________________

Building load factor ([*R/U*] – 1): ____________________

Efficiency ratio (*R/G*): ____________________

Building description: ____________________

Economic Data

	Actual	**Projected**	**Comments**
Potential gross income	______	______	____________
Other income	______	______	____________
Total *PGI*	______	______	____________
Vacancy and collection loss	______	______	____________
Effective gross income	______	______	____________
Expenses	______	______	____________
Net operating income	______	______	____________

Major/credit tenants: ____________________

Property interest conveyed: ❏ Fee simple ❏ Leased fee ❏ Leasehold

Sale Analysis

Price per sq. ft. rentable: ____________________

Overall capitalization rate: ____________________

EGIM: ____________________

Investor Expectations

Projection period: ____________________

Equity dividend rate: ____________________

Equity yield rate: ____________________

Miscellaneous Comments ____________________

____

____

____

Step 4. Organize Data and Calculate Units of Comparison

After confirming numerous comparable sales, listings, and contracts, the appraiser then selects and organizes the data for analysis. Step 3 generally produces more data than is actually used in the valuation process. As a result, not all the data and comparables confirmed in Step 3 are used in the valuation analysis. The confirmation process may have disclosed information about a comparable that prohibits its use in the appraisal. For example, during the confirmation process, the appraiser may have discovered that one or more of the transactions were not arm's-length in nature, meaning that they were sales to related parties. The appraiser selects those comparables that best represent the subject property in the contemporary market. Physical characteristics, location characteristics, and date of sale are primary variables for selecting comparables. Once the best comparables have been selected, the appraiser typically organizes the data on a summary grid and calculates the relevant units of comparison. An example of a summary grid is provided in Exhibit 6.2.

Step 5. Identify Value-Influencing Differences (Elements of Comparison)

In the sales comparison process, the appraiser must be able to efficiently determine which property and transaction characteristics have the greatest impact on value and then focus on these characteristics. In effect, appraisers should attempt to "mirror the market" by identifying the significant value-influencing characteristics of the property and the comparables. To assist appraisers in identifying value-influencing differences, real estate professionals have developed a list of 10 basic elements of comparison, based on decades of professional experience. These elements of comparison are

1. Real property rights conveyed
2. Financing terms
3. Conditions of sale
4. Expenditures made immediately after purchase
5. Market conditions (time)
6. Location
7. Physical characteristics
8. Economic characteristics
9. Use
10. Non-realty components of value

Exhibit 6.2 Summary Grid of Comparable Sales

Comparable	Subject	1	2	3	4	5
Sale price		$3,870,000	$5,200,000	$3,850,000	$3,450,000	$3,200,000
Price per sq. ft. (gross)		$122.86	$144.44	$128.33	$107.81	$110.34
Price per sq. ft. (rentable)		$135.01	$148.91	$142.59	$114.69	$125.39
Price per sq. ft. (usable)		$148.51	$166.78	$154.00	$127.31	$145.45
NOI per sq. ft. (gross)		$9.95	$11.99	$10.91	$9.60	$9.60
NOI per sq. ft. (rentable)		$10.94	$12.36	$12.12	$10.21	$10.91
NOI per sq. ft. (usable)		$12.03	$13.84	$13.09	$11.33	$12.65
Property rights conveyed	Leased fee	Leased fee	Leased fee	Leased fee	Below mkt.	Leased fee
Financing terms	Market	Market	Market	Favorable	Market	Market
Conditions of sale	Normal	Normal	Normal	Normal	Normal	Normal
Exp. made after purchase	None	None	None	None	None	None
Date of sale (market conditions)	Current date	2 mos. ago	12 mos. ago	6 mos. ago	8 mos. ago	13 mos. ago
Location	Good	Similar	Similar	Superior	Similar	Inferior
Physical characteristics						
Site area (sq. ft.)	104,575	98,438	112,500	85,714	106,667	107,407
Site utility	Good	Similar	Similar	Similar	Inferior	Similar
Gross building area (sq. ft.)	32,000	31,500	36,000	30,000	32,000	29,000
Rentable building area (sq. ft.)	29,120	28,665	34,920	27,000	30,080	25,520
Usable building area (sq. ft.)	26,000	26,059	31,179	25,000	27,099	22,000
Age/condition	5 yrs./good	8 yrs./good	1 yr./excell.	3 yrs./good	22 yrs./avg.	4 yrs./good
Parking ratio (stalls per 1,000 sq. ft.)	1.7	1.9	3	1.2	3.1	2.7
Land-to-bldg. ratio	3.27	3.13	3.13	2.86	3.33	3.70
Floor area ratio	31%	32%	32%	35%	30%	27%
Bldg. load factor	12%	10%	12%	8%	11%	16%
Efficiency ratio	91%	91%	97%	90%	94%	88%
Economic characteristics						
Overall capitalization rate		8.1%	8.3%	8.5%	8.9%	8.7%
Effective gross inc. multiplier		7.30	7.67	7.55	6.80	7.20

Real Property Rights Conveyed

Office properties with existing leases typically convey the leased fee interest, which is the landlord's interest, at the time of sale. If the leases are short term, the value of the leased fee interest and the fee simple interest may be very similar. However, if the leases are long term and the lease terms are different than market terms, the value of the leased fee interest may diverge from the fee simple interest. The appraiser must clearly understand the interest being appraised and then carefully assess each comparable to determine the interest conveyed. This can be one of the most important elements of comparison in the valuation of existing office properties, but it is frequently glossed over by appraisers. On a practical basis, the appraiser must

1. Obtain the lease terms from the subject property and the comparables
2. Compare the lease terms with market terms
3. Determine whether the lease terms influenced the transaction prices of the comparables, and
4. Adjust for differences, if applicable

When appraising the fee simple interest in a property, it would be preferable to use leased fee transactions with similar market rents. Conversely, it would be preferable to use leased fee transactions with similar lease terms when appraising the leased fee interest in a property. Differences between lease terms would of course require examination and possible adjustment.

Financing Terms

The definition of *market value* assumes an arm's-length transaction in which the buyer pays cash or offers terms equivalent to cash. In most acquisitions, buyers obtain financing from conventional lenders and then combine the debt (mortgage funds) with equity (down payment) to finalize the transaction. The financing terms provided by conventional lenders are considered to be "terms equivalent to cash." If the seller offers terms that are considered favorable to the buyer–i.e., below-market financing terms--the favorable financing has most likely inflated the purchase price. This would require that the appraiser assess the impact of favorable financing on the purchase price and make an appropriate adjustment.

Conditions of Sale

The conditions of sale relate to the arm's-length nature of the transaction and the motivations of both the buyer and the seller. If the buyer and seller are not related, the property has been exposed to the market for a reasonable period of time, and there are no unusual conditions of sale, it is assumed that the transaction is normal and no adjustment for this item is warranted. If, however, these assumptions are violated, the appraiser must either eliminate the transaction from the analysis or adequately investigate the unusual conditions of sale and make the necessary adjustments. On a practical basis, most appraisers will eliminate these types of sales from the analysis if other arm's-length transactions are available. However, in commercial markets, the scarcity of data sometimes requires that appraisers consider these transactions. In the current environment, conditions of sale may be impacted by numerous items, such as a 1031 tax-deferred exchange or a sale-leaseback transaction. It is incumbent upon the appraiser to carefully confirm the particulars of the transaction with knowledgeable parties, assess the conditions of sale, and make any necessary appropriate adjustments.

Expenditures Made Immediately After Purchase

Buyers of office properties occasionally incur extensive expenditures immediately after purchase due to atypical subject property characteristics. These expenditures may include the cost to cure deferred maintenance or the cost to remediate environmental contamination. *The Appraisal of Real Estate* notes that "the expenditures adjustment is included among the transactional adjustments because it reflects those items that a buyer would have considered part of the price at the time of sale."[2] This adjustment precedes the market conditions adjustment, whereas the conditions adjustment is handled later as one of the adjustments for physical characteristics.

Market Conditions (Time)

Because of the lack of transactions data in some commercial office markets, the appraiser is frequently obligated to use transactions that have occurred months or sometimes years prior to the date of valuation. In addition, the closing of commercial property transactions sometimes occurs many months after the execution of the sales contract. As a result, market or economic conditions may have changed significantly between the date of sale (contract date) and the date of valuation, requiring adjustment for changes in market conditions. Trends in rents, occupancies, and capitalization rates frequently provide a good indication of changing market conditions. Perhaps the best way to assess a change in market conditions between the date of sale and the date of valuation is to analyze a sale and resale of the same property during the period under consideration. Of course, one must be careful to ascertain that the variance in price is not due to factors other than changes in market conditions, such as a major renovation.

Location

A frequently used saying in the world of real estate is, "The three most important things about real estate are location, location, and location." This drives home the point that location, in and of itself, may have a consequen-

2. *The Appraisal of Real Estate*, 13th ed. (Chicago: Appraisal Institute, 2008), 331-332.

tial impact on property value. Therefore, location is typically one of the most important variables used in the selection of comparable sales for all types of real estate. Even if the other physical attributes of a property are identical, a significant difference in location may make the comparable sale unusable. Rents, occupancies, and capitalization rates frequently provide a good measure of comparability among office locations.

Physical Characteristics

The physical attributes of a property may significantly influence its rent, occupancy, and capitalization rates. These, of course, influence the value of the property and therefore must be carefully assessed in the sales comparison approach. Some of the more important physical characteristics in office properties include site area and utility; building age and condition; parking; story height; floor-area ratio; load factor; efficiency ratio; and gross, rentable, and usable square footage.

Economic Characteristics

The economic attributes of a property are those items that may influence its net operating income, such as rent concessions, lease terms, renewal options, expense recovery clauses, and tenant mix. Generally, economic conditions are homogeneous among similar office properties in close proximity. However, when the appraiser is obligated to use comparables in divergent locations and with varying physical characteristics, adjustments for economic attributes may be necessary. When this is the case, the appraiser should be sure to avoid double-counting the effect of locational differences. It is important to use caution in venturing down this path. Otherwise, the sales comparison approach may become just a variation of the income capitalization approach, which reduces the effectiveness of this alternative approach to value.

Use

Comparables that have similar uses are usually selected. No adjustments would be necessary in a case like this. However, *potential* uses may vary significantly in some jurisdictions, meaning that some office properties may have greater use or zoning rights than other office properties. If sales of such properties are used in the sales comparison approach, adjustments may be necessary to account for these differences. For instance, the zoning on a comparable sale may allow for a veterinary clinic. The scarcity of this use option in the municipality may increase the value of the property and would need to be addressed in the sales comparison approach. Generally, the appraiser can establish the use on a property by studying land zoning maps and confirming the findings with city zoning officials. Unusual findings must be carefully investigated to determine if the difference influenced the transaction price and if an adjustment for this item is warranted.

Non-Realty Components of Value

Periodically, an office property transaction includes non-realty items such as furniture, fixtures, and equipment (FF&E) or business/going concerns. The majority of office property transactions do not include non-realty components, and sales that do involve non-realty components are often those of smaller, owner-occupied office properties in which the proprietor includes the business, FF&E, and real estate in one package. When such a sale is discovered, most appraisers eliminate the transaction from the sales comparison approach. However, if the appraiser does decide to use the transaction, he or she must carefully examine and separate the respective parts and apply appropriate adjustments.

Step 6. Adjust for Differences

Qualitative Analysis

In qualitative analysis, the appraiser examines each value-influencing difference in comparison to its relative status to the subject property and determines if it is inferior, superior, or similar to the subject. Qualitative analysis recognizes the imperfections and inefficiencies in commercial markets and the practical difficulty of quantifying the differences that warrant adjustment.

Qualitative analysis attempts to estimate the market value of the subject property through a bracketing process. A unit of comparison, such as price per rentable square foot, is typically calculated from each comparable sale. Then, after discussing the relative comparison of each value-influencing difference, an overall comparison–such as "very superior," "superior," "slightly superior," and so on–is made to the subject property. This technique is most effective when the characteristics of the comparables clearly bracket those of the subject property. This bracketing process can lead to a clear inference of the subject's value.

The following case study illustrates the applicability of both qualitative and quantitative analysis techniques.

Elm Drive Case Study

The following table compares the Elm Drive office building to five comparable office buildings.

Elm Drive Office Building (Subject)

- 3-story, 5-yr.-old bldg. in good condition
- 32,000 gross sq. ft.
- 29,120 rentable sq. ft.
- 26,000 usable sq. ft.
- 95% occupied
- Good location
- Good site utility
- Parking ratio (stalls/1,000 sq. ft.): 1.7
- Floor area ratio (FAR): 31%
- Building load factor: 12%
- Efficiency ratio: 91%

Comparable 1

- Sold 2 mos. ago for $3,870,000
- 2-story, 8-yr.-old bldg. in good condition
- 31,500 gross sq. ft.
- 28,665 rentable sq. ft.
- 26,059 usable sq. ft.
- Fully leased at market rates
- Sold with market-level financing terms
- Normal conditions of sale
- No material expenditures made after purchase
- Good location
- Good site utility
- Parking ratio: 1.9
- FAR: 32%
- Building load factor: 10%
- Efficiency ratio: 91%

Comparable 2

- Sold 12 mos. ago for $5,200,000
- 3-story, 1-yr.-old bldg. in excellent condition
- 36,000 gross sq. ft.
- 34,920 rentable sq. ft.
- 31,179 usable sq. ft.
- 93% occupied, 5 tenants
- Sold with market-level financing terms
- Normal conditions of sale
- No material expenditures made after purchase
- Good location
- Good site utility
- Parking ratio: 3.0
- FAR: 32%
- Building load factor: 12%
- Efficiency ratio: 97%

Comparable 3

- Sold 6 mos. ago for $3,850,000 with favorable financing
- 2-story, 3-yr.-old bldg. in good condition
- 30,000 gross sq. ft.
- 27,000 rentable sq. ft.
- 25,000 usable sq. ft.
- 95% occupied, 6 tenants, market rates
- Seller carried back note at below-market rates and indicated that favorable financing inflated purchase price by $120,000
- Normal conditions of sale
- No material expenditures made after purchase
- Excellent location
- Good site utility
- Parking ratio: 1.2
- FAR: 35%
- Building load factor: 8%
- Efficiency ratio: 90%

Comparable 4

- Sold 8 mos. ago for $3,450,000
- 3-story, 22-yr.-old bldg. in average condition
- 32,000 gross sq. ft.
- 30,080 rentable sq. ft.
- 27,099 usable sq. ft.
- Occupied by 5 tenants, with 1 of the tenants holding a favorable long-term lease at a below-market rate
- Buyer indicated that he discounted the price by $150,000 due to the below-market lease
- Overall occupancy at time of sale: 97%
- Sold with market-level financing terms
- Normal conditions of sale
- No material expenditures made after purchase
- Good location
- Average site utility
- Significantly older than other comparables
- Parking ratio: 3.1
- FAR: 30%
- Building load factor: 11%
- Efficiency ratio: 94%

Comparable 5

- Sold 13 mos. ago for $3,200,000
- 2-story, 4-yr.-old bldg. in good condition
- 29,000 gross sq. ft.
- 25,520 rentable sq. ft.
- 22,000 usable sq. ft.
- Fully leased at market rates
- Sold with market-level financing terms
- Normal conditions of sale
- No material expenditures made after purchase
- Average location
- Good site utility
- Parking ratio: 2.7
- FAR: 27%
- Building load factor: 16%
- Efficiency ratio: 88%

Case Study Analysis

Exhibit 6.3 illustrates an adjustment grid using qualitative analysis. Comparables 4 and 2 provide the relevant range from $115 to $149 per square foot of rentable area. Comparable 2 is significantly superior to the subject property, while Comparable 4 is significantly inferior. Comparables 1 and 5 sold for $135 and $125 per square foot, respectively, and are considered slightly inferior. Comparable 3 sold for $143 per square foot and is considered slightly superior to the subject property. This analysis suggests that the value of the subject property lies between $135 and $143 per square foot. Based on this analysis, a value conclusion of approximately $140 per square foot is estimated. This provides a market value estimate for the subject property of $4,076,800 ($140 × 29,120 sq. ft.), rounded to $4,100,000.

Exhibit 6.3 Qualitative Adjustment Grid

Comparable	Subject	1	2	3	4	5
Sale price		$3,870,000	$5,200,000	$3,850,000	$3,450,000	$3,200,000
Gross square feet	32,000	31,500	36,000	30,000	32,000	29,000
Rentable square feet	29,120	28,665	34,920	27,000	30,080	25,520
Usable square feet	26,000	26,059	31,179	25,000	27,099	22,000
Price per rentable square foot		$135.01	$148.91	$142.59	$114.69	$125.39
Property rights conveyed	Leased fee	Leased fee	Leased fee	Leased fee	Below mkt.	Leased fee
Comparability		None	None	None	Upward	None
Financing terms	Market	Market	Market	Favorable	Market	Market
Comparability		None	None	Superior	None	None
Conditions of sale	Normal	Normal	Normal	Normal	Normal	Normal
Comparability		None	None	None	None	None
Exp. made after purchase	None	None	None	None	None	None
Comparability		None	None	None	None	None
Date of sale (market conditions)	Current date	2 mos. ago	12 mos. ago	6 mos. ago	8 mos. ago	13 mos. ago
Comparability		Inferior	Inferior	Inferior	Inferior	Inferior
Location	Good	Similar	Similar	Superior	Similar	Inferior
Comparability		None	None	Superior	None	Inferior
Physical characteristics						
Site utility	Good	Similar	Similar	Similar	Inferior	Similar
Comparability		None	None	None	Inferior	None
Gross building area (sq. ft.)	32,000	31,500	36,000	30,000	32,000	29,000
Comparability		None	Inferior	None	None	None
Age/condition	5 yrs./good	8 yrs./good	1 yr./excell.	3 yrs./good	22 yrs./avg.	4 yrs./good
Comparability		None	Superior	None	Inferior	None
Parking ratio (stalls per 1,000 sq. ft.)	1.7	1.9	3.0	1.2	3.1	2.7
Comparability		None	Superior	Inferior	Superior	Superior
Floor area ratio (FAR)	31%	32%	32%	35%	30%	27%
Comparability		None	None	Inferior	None	Superior
Bldg. load factor ($R/U - 1$)	12%	10%	12%	8%	11%	16%
Comparability		None	None	Superior	None	Inferior
Efficiency ratio (R/G)	91%	91%	97%	90%	94%	88%
Comparability		None	Superior	None	Superior	Inferior
Overall comparability		Slightly inferior	Superior	Slightly superior	Inferior	Slightly inferior

Quantitative Analysis

Frequently, clients expect the appraiser to estimate the magnitude of the value-influencing differences by quantifying the adjustments. In some cases, the magnitude of the adjustments can be estimated empirically, but in many cases the adjustments are estimated based on the experience and judgment of the appraiser. When making quantitative adjustments, the appraiser must take care not to mislead the intended users of the report by inferring a level of precision or supporting data and analysis that do not exist. Quantitative adjustments take the form of percentages, dollar amounts, or both. The order of the adjustments is determined by the appraiser's analysis of the data.[3]

When applying percentage adjustments, the appraiser must be careful in the application. For instance, when adjusting the comparable to the subject (the typical case), the percentage adjustment must be correctly applied, as follows:

$$P_C = \text{Price of the comparable}$$

$$V_S = \text{Value of the subject}$$

$$\%\text{Adj} = \text{Percent of adjustment}$$

When the comparable is inferior to the subject, the calculation is

$$V_S = \left(\frac{P_C}{1 - \%\text{Adj}}\right)$$

If the comparable is superior to the subject, the calculation is

$$V_S = \left(\frac{P_C}{1 + \%\text{Adj}}\right)$$

For example, assume that the comparable sold for $3,700,000 and that it is considered to be 10% inferior to the subject property.

Using the previous equation, the calculation would be:

$$V_S = \left(\frac{\$3,700,000}{1 - 0.10}\right) = \$4,111,111$$

Similarly, assume that the comparable was 10% superior to the subject property. In this case,

$$V_S = \left(\frac{\$3,700,000}{1 + 0.10}\right) = \$3,363,636$$

Elm Drive Case Study, Continued

Exhibit 6.4 illustrates the application of quantified adjustments in the sales comparison approach for the Elm Drive office building.

3. *The Appraisal of Real Estate* prescribes a general sequence of adjustments, which is the first five "transactional" adjustments in order followed by the five "property" adjustments in any order.

Exhibit 6.4 Quantitative Adjustment Grid

Comparable	Subject	1	2	3	4	5
Sale price		$3,870,000	$5,200,000	$3,850,000	$3,450,000	$3,200,000
Gross square feet	32,000	31,500	36,000	30,000	32,000	29,000
Rentable square feet	29,120	28,665	34,920	27,000	30,080	25,520
Usable square feet	26,000	26,059	31,179	25,000	27,099	22,000
Price per rentable square foot		$135.01	$148.91	$142.59	$114.69	$125.39
Property rights conveyed	Leased fee	Leased fee	Leased fee	Leased fee	Below mkt.	Leased fee
Adjustment ($)		$0	$0	$0	+$150,000	$0
Adjusted sale price		$3,870,000	$5,200,000	$3,850,000	$3,600,000	$3,200,000
Financing terms	Market	Market	Market	Favorable	Market	Market
Adjustment ($)		$0	$0	-$120,000	$0	$0
Adjusted sale price		$3,870,000	$5,200,000	$3,730,000	$3,600,000	$3,200,000
Conditions of sale	Normal	Normal	Normal	Normal	Normal	Normal
Adjustment ($)		$0	$0	$0	$0	$0
Adjusted sale price		$3,870,000	$5,200,000	$3,730,000	$3,600,000	$3,200,000
Exp. made after purchase	None	None	None	None	None	None
Adjustment ($)		$0	$0	$0	$0	$0
Adj. price per rentable sq. ft.		$135.01	$148.91	$138.15	$119.68	$125.39
Date of sale (market conditions)	Current	2 mos. ago	12 mos. ago	6 mos. ago	8 mos. ago	13 mos. ago
Adjustment (%)		+0.50%	+3.00%	+1.50%	+2.00%	+3.25%
Adj. price per rentable sq. ft.		$135.69	$153.38	$140.22	$122.07	$129.47
Location	Good	Good	Good	Excellent	Good	Average
Adjustment (%)		0%	0%	-5%	0	+5%
Adj. price per rentable sq. ft.		$135.69	$153.38	$133.21	$122.07	$135.94
Physical characteristics						
Site utility	Good	Good	Good	Good	Average	Good
Adjustment (%)		0%	0%	0%	+5%	0%
Gross building area (sq. ft.)	32,000	31,500	36,000	30,000	32,000	29,000
Adjustment (%)		0%	+5%	0%	0%	0%
Age/condition	5 yrs./good	8 yrs./good	1 yr./excell.	3 yrs./good	22 yrs./avg.	4 yrs./good
Adjustment (%)		0%	-5%	0%	+10%	0%
Parking ratio (stalls per 1,000 sq. ft.)	1.7	1.9	3.0	1.2	3.1	2.7
Adjustment (%)		0%	-10%	+5%	-10%	-5%
Floor area ratio (FAR)	31%	32%	32%	35%	30%	27%
Adjustment (%)		0%	0%	+5%	0%	-5%
Bldg. load factor (*R*/*U* – 1)	12%	10%	12%	8%	11%	16%
Adjustment (%)		0%	0%	-5%	0%	+5%
Efficiency ratio (R/G)	91%	91%	97%	90%	94%	88%
Adjustment (%)		0%	-5%	0%	-2%	+2%
Total net adj. for physical characteristics*		0%	-14.71%	+4.74%	+1.87%	-3.34%
Total adj. price per rentable sq. ft.		$136	$131	$140	$124	$131
Total net adjustment (%)		0.50%	-12.16%	-2.16%	8.43%	4.79%
Total gross adjustment (%)		0.50%	31.16%	27.22%	37.93%	28.01%

* Total net adjustment for physical characteristics has been calculated by converting percentage adjustments to whole numbers (for example, +10% becomes 1.10) and multiplying all adjustments for physical characteristics.

The appraiser typically summarizes the analysis from the adjustment grid in a narrative format in the appraisal report and provides any empirical analysis or supporting data that may be available. After completing the adjustment process as shown in Exhibit 6.4, the appraiser summarizes the results and concludes with a final estimate of value. For example, the previous analysis is summarized in Exhibit 6.5.

Exhibit 6.5 Summary of Adjusted Price per Square Foot

Comparable	**1**	**2**	**3**	**4**	**5**
Price per rentable sq. ft. prior to adjustment	$135.01	$148.91	$142.59	$114.69	$125.39
Total net adjustment (%)	0.50%	-12.16%	-2.16%	8.43%	4.79%
Total adjusted price per rentable sq. ft.	$136	$131	$140	$124	$131

Prior to adjustment, the prices ranged from $115 to $149 per square foot. After the adjustments, the range was narrowed considerably to $124 to $140 per square foot. Comparables 2 and 4 required the greatest percentage of adjustment, so less weight is placed on them. The remaining comparables range from $131 to $140 per square foot. Comparables 1 ($136) and 3 ($140) required little net adjustment, suggesting that considerable weight be placed on these comparables. Based on this analysis, a value of $4,018,560 ($138 × 29,120 sq. ft.) is estimated, rounded to $4,000,000.

Step 7. Reconcile the Analysis

In both of the previous cases (qualitative analysis and quantitative adjustment), the reconciliation process took the form of evaluating the characteristics of the comparable properties with respect to the subject property. The greatest weight was placed on the data that was considered most representative of the subject property. If multiple techniques were used, the appraiser would evaluate the reliability of the respective techniques and consider the weight that market participants place on it. In this process, it is important that the appraiser continually look to the market by considering the perspectives of buyers and sellers. The appraiser must then apply these perspectives to the data and analysis in arriving at a final estimate of value.

Alternative Valuation Scenarios

The Elm Drive Case Study illustrated the application of the sales comparison approach for estimating the "as is" market value of the leased fee interest of an office property at stabilized occupancy. Two common alternative valuation scenarios include the "as is" market value of the fee simple interest at stabilized occupancy and the market value of the fee simple interest when complete. These alternative valuation scenarios are discussed here in the context of the sales comparison approach.

Valuation Scenario 2

In Valuation Scenario 2, the property interest appraised is fee simple, the property status is "as is," and the occupancy status is stabilized. Assuming that the property and occupancy status are the same (i.e., "as is" and stabilized), the leased fee and fee simple interests are distinguished by the difference between market rental rates and terms and contract rental rates and terms. If the appraiser finds that the market rental rates and terms are similar to the contract rental rates and terms, the market value of the leased fee interest and that of the fee simple interest are the same. However, the market values of the respective interests will be different if the rates and terms are different. If the subject property's contract rental rates and terms are inferior to the market rental rates and terms, the market value of the leased fee interest will be lower than the market value of the fee simple interest. Conversely, if the subject property has above-market lease terms, the market value of the leased fee interest will be higher than the market value of the fee simple interest. In this latter case, the appraiser must carefully analyze the creditworthiness of the lease(s) and estimate the probability that the tenant(s) will honor the lease(s) because the tenants may have a financial incentive to default on the lease and move to office space that offers more favorable lease terms.

When estimating the market value of the fee simple interest, the appraiser must analyze each comparable and determine if the contract lease terms are similar to market terms. If so, there would be no adjustment for property rights appraised. However, if the lease terms differ from market value, an adjustment may be warranted.

For example, assume that market rental rates were $20 per square foot on an absolute net lease basis. Also assume that market lease rates escalate at 3% per year and are typically written for five-year terms. Assume that a comparable sold for $135 per square foot and had a below-market lease at $18.50 per square foot that would escalate at 3% per year with three years remaining. Also assume that a 10% yield rate (discount rate) was frequently used on office properties in the current market. Based on this information, the adjustment to the comparable would be calculated as follows:

Year	1	2	3
Market rents/sq. ft.	$20.00	$20.60	$21.22
Contract rents/sq. ft.	$18.50	$19.06	$19.63
Difference	$1.50	$1.54	$1.59

Discounting the rent differences over the three years at 10% results in $3.83 per square foot. Therefore, an upward adjustment of $3.83 per square foot would be applied to the comparable as follows:

	$135.00	Sale Price per Square Foot
+	3.83	Adjustment for Property Rights
	$138.83	Adjusted Price per Square Foot

The result is a market value estimate of the fee simple interest of the subject property. If the contract rents of the comparable were above market levels, a similar methodology would be employed, but the resulting adjustment would be deducted from the transaction price of the comparable to estimate the fee simple interest in the subject property.

Valuation Scenario 3

The property interest appraised is fee simple, the property status is "when complete," and the occupancy status is vacant. The difference between the value as vacant and as stabilized consists of the present value of the net operating income losses that occur during the interim period. For instance, assume that an office building, when complete, will take three years to achieve stabilized occupancy. Also assume that the *NOI* losses are estimated as follows:

Year	1	2	3
NOI (stabilized)	$355,000	$360,000	$365,000
Forecast *NOI*	$55,000	$275,000	$365,000
Loss	$300,000	$85,000	0
Leasing commissions	$20,000	$21,000	$23,000
Tenant improvements	$40,000	$42,000	$44,000
Total loss	$360,000	$148,000	$67,000

Next, assume that a 10% discount rate is applicable and that the present value of the loss is $499,924, rounded to $500,000. The value of the property when complete is calculated by deducting the present value of the loss from the value at stabilized occupancy as follows:

	$4,000,000	Market Value, Fee Simple, Stabilized
–	500,000	Present Value of *NOI* Losses
	$3,500,000	Market Value, Fee Simple, When Complete

In this example, a discount rate of 10% was used to discount the rent loss. This is the same rate that was used when discounting the cash flows before debt service and reversion to arrive at a value estimate for the Maple Landing Case Study property. It is very important that the appraiser select the discount rate that is adequately supported in the market. A survey of market participants may be very helpful in this situation. It is also important that the appraiser understand the relationship between discount rates used for stabilized projections, lease-up projections, and rent loss projections. If the discount rate for a lease-up projection is higher than the discount rate for a stabilized projection (to reflect the higher risk during the lease-up period), the discount rate for the rent loss projection will be lower than the discount rates used for stabilized and lease-up projections. This is shown in the following example.

Assume that the "stabilized" projection of *NOI* and reversion are forecast as follows:

Year	1	2	3	4	5
NOI	$355,000	$360,000	$365,000	$370,000	$375,000
Reversion					$4,285,000
Discount rate: 10%	0.90909	0.82645	0.75131	0.68301	0.62092
Present value	$ 322,727	$ 297,521	$ 274,230	$ 252,715	$2,893,493

Note: Calculations may vary due to rounding.

Property value = $4,040,686

Assume that the lease-up projection of *NOI* and reversion are as follows:

Year	1	2	3	4	5
NOI	$55,000	$275,000	$365,000	$370,000	$375,000
Reversion					$4,285,000
Discount rate: 11% for Years 1 & 2, 10% for Years 3-5	0.90090	0.81162	0.75131	0.68301	0.62092
Present value	$49,550	$223,196	$274,230	$252,715	$2,893,493

Note: Calculations may vary due to rounding.

Property value = $3,693,184

The difference in value is $347,502. The *NOI* loss for each period is calculated as follows:

Year	1	2	3	4	5
NOI loss	$300,000	$ 85,000	-	-	-

The value and the rent loss differentials for each period are shown as follows:

Year	0	1	2	3	4	5
Cash flows	($347,502)	$300,000	$ 85,000	-	-	-
IRR	8.81%					

Therefore, the discount rate used to calculate the value of the loss will always be lower if the discount rate for the lease-up projection is higher than the discount rate for the stabilized projection.

Chapter 7

The Cost Approach

The cost approach is an appraisal technique which assumes that a rational and prudent purchaser will pay no more for a property than the cost of reproducing or replacing a similar property with the same utility. The cost approach is formally defined as a set of procedures through which a value indication is derived for the fee simple interest in a property by estimating the current cost to construct a reproduction of (or replacement for) the existing structure, including an entrepreneurial incentive, deducting the depreciation from the total cost, and adding the estimated land value. Adjustments may then be made to the indicated fee simple value of the subject property to reflect the value of the property interest being appraised.[1]

Estimating a property's value via the cost approach involves six steps.

1. Site valuation
   Estimate the value of the subject property's site as though vacant and at its highest and best use.
2. Reproduction or replacement cost
   Estimate the reproduction or replacement cost new of all building improvements by identifying all direct and indirect costs, including entrepreneurial profit.
3. Depreciation
   Estimate all elements of accrued depreciation, including physical deterioration, functional obsolescence, and external obsolescence.
4. Subtract total depreciation from building improvements
   Subtract the total accrued depreciation from the reproduction or replacement cost new of the building improvements. This step provides the depreciated cost new of the building improvements.
5. Estimate and add the depreciated cost new of the site improvements.
6. Conclusion of value
   Add the estimated site value to the depreciated cost new of the improvements.

---

1. All definitions of terms in this chapter are taken from *The Dictionary of Real Estate Appraisal*, 4th ed. (Chicago: Appraisal Institute, 2002).

Each step is discussed in this chapter.

Step 1. Site Valuation

Site valuation is typically accomplished by using the techniques outlined in the sales comparison approach. First, the appraiser identifies the attributes of the subject's site and then searches all applicable sources for comparable sales of similar parcels. Second, the appraiser identifies value-influencing differences between the subject's site and the comparable sales and adjusts for these differences. Third, the appraiser reconciles the adjusted prices of the comparable sales and concludes to an estimate of value.

The appraiser typically organizes the land sales information for comparables on data sheets such as the one shown in Exhibit 7.1.

Exhibit 7.1 Land Sale Comparable Data Sheet

Land comparable no. ____________________

Property Identification

Type: ____________________
Location/address: ____________________
Tax parcel no.: ____________________

Sale Data

Sale price: ____________________
Financing terms: ____________________
Unit value: ____________________
Sale date: ____________________
Recording date: ____________________
Grantor: ____________________
Grantee: ____________________
Instrument: ____________________
Listing price: ____________________
Listing date: ____________________
Days on market: ____________________
Confirmation: ____________________

Site Data

Shape/dimensions: ____________________
Area: ____________________
Zoning ordinance/restrictions: ____________________
Traffic count: ____________________
Frontage: ____________________
Legal access: ____________________
Visibility: ____________________
Topography: ____________________
Utilities available: ____________________
Off-site improvements: ____________________

Comments

____
____
____
____

Once the comparable sales are identified and confirmed, the appraiser organizes the data and computes an adjustment grid like the one shown in Exhibit 7.2.

Exhibit 7.2 Land Sales Adjustment Grid

	Subject	Comp 1	Comp 2	Comp 3	Comp 4	Comp 5
Sale price		$575,000	$535,000	$1,770,000	$250,000	$310,000
Sale price per sq. ft.		$9.57	$11.37	$10.08	$10.43	$10.62
Property rights conveyed	Fee simple	Fee simple	Fee simple	Fee simple	Fee simple	Fee simple
Adjustment		0%	0%	0%	0%	0%
Financing terms	Cash/mkt.	Market	Cash	Cash	Market	Cash
Adjustment		0%	0%	0%	0%	0%
Conditions of sale	Normal	Normal	Normal	Normal	Normal	Normal
Adjustment		0%	0%	0%	0%	0%
Market conditions (time)	Current	Current	20 mos. ago	21 mos. ago	1 yr. ago	Current
Adjustment		0%	10%	10%	5%	0%
Location	Good	Same	Superior	Superior	Similar	Similar
Adjustment		0%	-20%	-20%	0%	0%
Size (acres)	1.49	1.38	1.08	4.03	0.55	0.67
Adjustment		0%	-5%	15%	-10%	-10%
Shape	Rectangular	Inferior	Similar	Similar	Similar	Inferior
Adjustment		5%	0%	0%	0%	5%
Topography	Level	Same	Same	Same	Same	Same
Adjustment		0%	0%	0%	0%	0%
Zoning/use	CBD	CBD	CBD	CBD	C-1	CBD
Adjustment		0%	0%	0%	5%	0%
Net adjustment		5%	-15%	5%	0%	-5%
Adjusted price per sq. ft.		$10.07	$9.89	$10.61	$10.43	$10.12

As noted in the previous chapter on the sales comparison approach, the appraiser concludes to a final opinion of value through a reconciliation process. In this instance, the appraiser may conclude to $10 per square foot, or $649,040 ($10 × 64,904 sq. ft.), rounded to $650,000.

If the appraiser is unable to find comparable land sales, he or she must either employ an alternative valuation technique–such as an extraction method or a land residual technique–or consider abandoning the cost approach as a reliable method for estimating the value of the subject's site.[2]

Step 2. Reproduction or Replacement Cost

For the second step in the cost approach, the appraiser estimates the reproduction or replacement cost of the building improvements. *Reproduc-*

2. Procedures for applying alternative techniques for estimating site value, such as the extraction method or land residual method, can be found in *The Appraisal of Real Estate*, 13th ed.

tion cost is the estimated cost to construct, at current prices and as of the effective date of the appraisal, an exact duplicate or replica of the building being appraised using the same materials, construction standards, design, layout, and quality of workmanship, and embodying all the deficiencies, superadequacies, and obsolescence of the subject building.

For newer office properties with contemporary building designs and construction materials, estimating the reproduction cost is preferred. However, for older properties with outdated designs and materials, estimating the reproduction cost may be challenging because of the difficulty in estimating current costs. In such cases, estimating replacement cost may be preferred. *Replacement cost* is the estimated cost to construct, at current prices as of the effective appraisal date, a building with utility equivalent to the building being appraised using modern materials and current standards, design, and layout.

The replacement cost approach focuses on the utility of the building rather than attempting to recreate an exact replica. Focusing on utility overcomes some forms of obsolescence, but it could be argued that the cost approach may be the least applicable approach for estimating value if the subject office building is older and suffers from significant obsolescence.

A comprehensive discussion regarding all the nuances of the cost approach is beyond the scope of this chapter, and the appraiser is encouraged to study other references on this topic.[3] Because the cost approach is most applicable and used most frequently for contemporary office buildings with modern designs and construction materials, this section will discuss the techniques for estimating the reproduction cost of such an office property.

For illustrative purposes, the Maple Landing Case Study property referred to in Chapter 5 will also be used here. The three-story office building has 32,100 square feet of gross area and underwent a major renovation two years ago. The building was originally constructed in 1979, and its actual age is about 30 years; however, considering the major renovation, the effective age is considered to be about 15 years.

There are three alternative methods for estimating the reproduction cost of an office building.

1. The comparative-unit method
2. The segregated (unit-in-place) method
3. The quantity survey method

These methods are listed in ascending order of detail and complexity.

Comparative-Unit Method

The comparative-unit method is a method used to derive a cost estimate in terms of dollars per unit of area or volume based on known costs of

3. Please refer to the Bibliography at the end of this book.

similar structures that are adjusted for time and physical differences. This method is usually applied to total building area. In the appraisal of office properties, this definition is understood to mean that the appraiser researches the typical cost per square foot of similar office properties in the local area and in the current period. This is best done by researching the total construction cost from recently completed or under-construction office buildings in the near vicinity of the subject property by talking with the owners and contractors of these properties. In some markets, third-party firms research and compile permit and construction cost data on new projects and sell this data to interested parties. Appraisers must confirm third-party data prior to using it in an appraisal report, but these services can provide excellent leads for obtaining reliable construction cost data.

In the comparative-unit process, it is very important that the appraiser select properties that are most similar in terms of size and quality. Construction costs on a "per unit" basis tend to go down with size. As a result, size is considered one of the most important variables in estimating reliable construction costs. The quality of the materials can also significantly impact construction costs. In short, primary research may result in a summary table of construction costs for comparable properties, as shown in Exhibit 7.3.

Exhibit 7.3 Example of the Comparative-Unit Method (Primary Research)

Construction Characteristics	Comparable 1	Comparable 2	Comparable 3
Building size (gross square feet)	26,500	32,300	29,700
Direct costs	$3,278,063.00	$3,982,009.00	$3,520,690.00
Indirect costs (including contractor's profit)	$204,633.00	$294,964.00	$280,791.00
Developer's profit	$452,554.00	$639,088.00	$518,384.00
Total reproduction cost	$3,935,250.00	$4,916,061.00	$4,319,865.00
Total reproduction cost per square foot	$148.50	$152.20	$145.45

After researching and analyzing the primary construction cost data, the appraiser evaluates the applicability of the data as it relates to the subject property and concludes to an estimate of total reproduction cost for the subject property. Assuming the appraiser concludes to $150 per square foot, the reproduction cost would be $4,815,000 (32,100 sq. ft. × $150 per sq. ft.).

Appraisers can, and frequently do, obtain construction cost data from cost-estimating services. The more prominent national cost-estimating services include

- Marshall & Swift: *www.marshallswift.com*
- Dodge: *www.fwdodge.com*
- RSMeans: *www.rsmeans.com*

Under the comparative-unit method, these services provide a range of unit costs–i.e., per square meter or per square foot–based on construction class as well as exterior and interior construction characteristics. For instance, Marshall & Swift provides a matrix of construction costs per unit based on construction class and type, exterior walls, and interior finish, as well as lighting, plumbing, mechanical, and heating systems. The appraiser usually selects the construction class and type by examining photographs and descriptions of existing office properties provided by Marshall & Swift. This selection results in a base unit cost. Exhibit 7.4 provides an example of the matrix of unit costs.

Exhibit 7.4 Example of the Calculator Method for Office Buildings, Marshall & Swift

Class	Type	Exterior Walls	Interior Finish	Lighting, Plumbing, and Mechanical	Heat	Sq. Ft.
B	Excellent	Best metal or stone, brick or block backup, tinted glass	Plaster, best veneers, vinyl wall coverings, vinyl, terrazzo, carpet	Luminous ceilings, many outlets, many private restrooms	Hot and chilled water (zoned)	$216.08
	Good	Good metal and solar glass, face brick, precast concrete panels	Drywall/plaster, some wall cover, acoustic tile, vinyl tile, carpet	Good high-intensity fluorescent lighting	Hot and chilled water (zoned) restrooms	$170.06
	Average	Brick, concrete, or metal and glass panels, little trim	Average partitions, acoustic tile, vinyl composition, some extras	Average-intensity fluorescent lighting, average restrooms	Warm and cool air (zoned)	$127.24
	Low cost	Minimum-cost walls and fenestration, little trim	Drywall, acoustic ceilings, asphalt tile, few partitions	Minimum office lighting and plumbing	Warm and cool air (zoned)	$100.86

Source: Marshall & Swift's *Marshall Valuation Service*. Reprinted with the permission of Marshall & Swift and its licensors, copyright 2007. May not be reprinted, copied, or automated without permission.

Once the applicable base cost is selected, adjustments are then made for the story height, sprinklers, elevators, canopy, building perimeter, and local market conditions, as shown in Exhibit 7.5. Applying the unit cost to the building area results in a total reproduction cost of the office building of $4,797,345 ($149.45 × 32,100 sq. ft.), rounded to $4,800,000.

Unit-in-Place Method (Segregated Cost)

The unit-in-place method is a cost-estimating method in which total building cost is estimated by adding together the unit costs for the various building components as installed. This method is also called the *segregated cost method.*

The unit-in-place method effectively segregates the major construction components of the office building and provides a unit cost for each. The unit measure for office properties is typically cost per square foot. A summation of all the segregated costs results in an estimate of the total reproduction cost of the office building. Because each major construction component is being estimated separately, the unit-in-place method can

Exhibit 7.5 Example of the Comparative-Unit Method for an Office Building

Base cost per sq. ft. (Class B construction, average type)	$127.24*
Adjustment for story height (0.5% for each story, 3 stories)	× 1.015
Adjusted cost per square foot	$129.15
Adjustment for floor area and perimeter	× 0.965
Adjusted cost per square foot	$124.63
Adjustment for current costs	× 1.05
Adjusted cost per square foot	$130.86
Adjustment for local costs	× 0.99
Adjusted cost per square foot	$129.55
Adjustment for indirect costs not included in base	× 1.03
Adjusted cost per square foot	$133.44
Adjustment for entrepreneurial profit	× 1.12
Total reproduction cost new per square foot	$149.45

* "Calculator costs are averages of final costs, including architects' fees and contractors' overhead and profit, sales taxes, permit fees, and insurance during construction. Interest on interim construction financing is also included, but not financing costs, real estate taxes, or brokerage commissions" (*Marshall Valuation Service*, Section 15, p. 1).

result in a more precise and defensible estimate of construction cost. However, the complexity involved in this method requires that the appraiser fully understand the intricacies of each construction component as well as all assumptions and nuances employed by the cost-estimating service. In practice, most appraisers prefer the comparative-unit method over the unit-in-place method; however, many appraisers also recognize that the latter technique provides a more complete picture of the construction components of the office building, thus leading to a more reliable estimate of value. An example of the unit-in-place method is provided in Exhibit 7.6.

The total building cost estimate includes all direct and indirect costs, but it does not include entrepreneurial or developer's profit. As a result, the appraiser would need to conduct market research to estimate this item and add it to the calculated total building cost to arrive at an estimate of the total reproduction cost of the office building. For example, assuming that the typical entrepreneurial profit in the current market was 12%, the total reproduction cost of the office building would be $4,599,840 ($4,107,000 × 1.12), rounded to $4,600,000.

Quantity Survey Method

The quantity survey method is a cost-estimating method in which the quantity and quality of all materials used and all categories of labor required are estimated and unit cost figures are applied to arrive at a total cost estimate for labor and materials.

For all intents and purposes, the quantity survey method attempts to replicate the general contractor's cost estimating process. Appraisers are very rarely expected to produce a quantity survey method independently. If this method is required by the client, perhaps for feasibility purposes,

Exhibit 7.6 RSMeans Cost Estimate

Square Foot Cost Estimate Report

Estimate Name:	**Untitled**
Building Type:	**Office, 2-4 Story with Glass and Metal Curtain Wall / Steel Frame**
Location:	**PHOENIX, AZ**
Story Count:	**3**
Story Height (L.F.):	**12**
Floor Area (S.F.):	**32100**
Labor Type:	**Union**
Basement Included:	**No**
Data Release:	**Year 2008 Quarter 1**
Cost Per Square Foot:	**$127.94**
Building Cost:	**$4,107,000**

Costs are derived from a building model with basic components.

Scope differences and market conditions can cause costs to vary significantly.

		% of Total	Cost Per S.F.	Cost
A Substructure		4.20%	$4.41	$141,500
A1010	**Standard Foundations**		**$1.92**	**$61,500**
	KSF, 12" deep x 24" wide			
	- 0" square x 20" deep			
	- 6" square x 25" deep			
A1030	**Slab on Grade**		**$1.40**	**$45,000**
	Slab on grade, 4" thick, non industrial, reinforced			
A2010	**Basement Excavation**		**$0.06**	**$2,000**
	storage			
A2020	**Basement Walls**		**$1.03**	**$33,000**
	thick			
	thick			
B Shell		34.80%	$36.14	$1,160,000
B1010	**Floor Construction**		**$12.35**	**$396,500**
	column, 25'x25' bay, 26" deep, 75 PSF superimposed load, 120 PSF total			
	column, 25'x25' bay, 26" deep, 75 PSF superimposed load, 120 PSF total			
	hour rating, 22 PLF			
B1020	**Roof Construction**		**$2.77**	**$89,000**
	20" deep, 40 PSF superimposed load, 60 PSF total load			
	20" deep, 40 PSF superimposed load, 60 PSF total load, add for column			
B2020	**Exterior Windows**		**$18.68**	**$599,500**
	Windows, aluminum, awning, insulated glass, 4'-5" x 5'-3"			
	opening, no intermediate horizontals			
	Glazing panel, insulating, 5/8" thick units, 2 lites 3/16" float glass, tinted			
B2030	**Exterior Doors**		**$0.76**	**$24,500**
	hardware, 6'-0" x 10'-0" opening			
	0" opening			
	opening			
B3010	**Roof Coverings**		**$1.57**	**$50,500**
	mopped			
	Insulation, rigid, roof deck, composite with 2" EPS, 1" perlite			
	Roof edges, aluminum, duranodic, .050" thick, 6" face			
	Flashing, aluminum, no backing sides, .019"			
	Gravel stop, aluminum, extruded, 4", duranodic, .050" thick			

Exhibit 7.6 **RSMeans Cost Estimate *(continued)***

C Interiors		22.60%	$23.46	$753,000
C1010	**Partitions**		**$2.29**	**$73,500**
	5/8" @ 24" OC framing ,same opposite face, no insulation			
	1/2" fire ratedgypsum board, taped & finished, painted on metal furring			
C1020	**Interior Doors**		**$3.93**	**$126,000**
	0" x 7'-0" x 1-3/8"			
C1030	**Fittings**		**$0.97**	**$31,000**
	Toilet partitions, cubicles, ceiling hung, plastic laminate			
C2010	**Stair Construction**		**$4.05**	**$130,000**
	Stairs, steel, cement filled metal pan & picket rail, 16 risers, with landing			
C3010	**Wall Finishes**		**$0.84**	**$27,000**
	& 2 coats			
	Vinyl wall covering, fabric back, medium weight			
C3020	**Floor Finishes**		**$6.64**	**$213,000**
	Carpet, tufted, nylon, roll goods, 12' wide, 36 oz			
	Carpet, padding, add to above, minimum			
	Vinyl, composition tile, maximum			
	Tile, ceramic natural clay			
C3030	**Ceiling Finishes**		**$4.75**	**$152,500**
	channel grid, suspended support			
D Services		38.50%	$39.98	$1,283,500
D1010	**Elevators and Lifts**		**$9.45**	**$303,500**
	group,125 FPM			
D2010	**Plumbing Fixtures**		**$1.60**	**$51,500**
	Water closet, vitreous china, bowl only with flush valve, wall hung			
	Urinal, vitreous china, wall hung			
	Lavatory w/trim, vanity top, PE on CI, 20" x 18"			
	Service sink w/trim, PE on CI, corner floor, wall hung w/rim guard, 24" x 20"			
	Water cooler, electric, wall hung, 8.2 GPH			
	Water cooler, electric, wall hung, wheelchair type, 7.5 GPH			
D2020	**Domestic Water Distribution**		**$0.17**	**$5,500**
	Gas fired water heater, commercial, 100< F rise, 240 MBH input, 230 GPH			
D2040	**Rain Water Drainage**		**$0.17**	**$5,500**
	Roof drain, CI, soil,single hub, 4" diam, 10' high			
	Roof drain, CI, soil,single hub, 4" diam, for each additional foot add			
D3050	**Terminal & Package Units**		**$14.28**	**$458,500**
	Rooftop, multizone, air conditioner, offices, 25,000 SF, 79.16 ton			
D4020	**Standpipes**		**$0.48**	**$15,500**
	Wet standpipe risers, class I, steel, black, sch 40, 4" diam pipe, 1 floor			
	floors			
D5010	**Electrical Service/Distribution**		**$2.32**	**$74,500**
	phase, 4 wire, 120/208 V, 1000 A			
	Feeder installation 600 V, including RGS conduit and XHHW wire, 1000 A			
	Switchgear installation, incl switchboard, panels & circuit breaker, 1200 A			
D5020	**Lighting and Branch Wiring**		**$7.80**	**$250,500**
	with transformer			
	Miscellaneous power, 1.2 watts			
	Central air conditioning power, 4 watts			
	Motor installation, three phase, 460 V, 15 HP motor size			
	fixtures @40 watt per 1000 SF			
D5030	**Communications and Security**		**$3.49**	**$112,000**
	Telephone wiring for offices & laboratories, 8 jacks/MSF			
	wire, fire detection systems, 25 detectors			
	Internet wiring, 8 data/voice outlets per 1000 S.F.			
D5090	**Other Electrical Systems**		**$0.20**	**$6,500**
	gas/gasoline operated, 3 phase, 4 wire, 277/480 V, 7.5 kW			
	Uninterruptible power supply with standard battery pack, 15 kVA/12.75 kW			

Exhibit 7.6 RSMeans Cost Estimate *(continued)*

E Equipment & Furnishings		0.00%	$0.00	$0
E1090	Other Equipment		$0.00	$0
F Special Construction		0.00%	$0.00	$0
G Building Sitework		0.00%	$0.00	$0

SubTotal	100%	$103.99	$3,338,000
Contractor Fees (General Conditions,Overhead,Profit)	15.00%	$15.59	$500,500
Architectural Fees	7.00%	$8.36	$268,500
User Fees	0.00%	$0.00	$0
Total Building Cost		$127.94	$4,107,000

Source: RSMeans CostWorks Online Square Foot Estimator, 2008. Copyright Reed Construction Data, Kingston, MA, 781-585-7880. *www.meanscostworks.com*.

the appraiser will often collaborate with and seek assistance from a general contractor who has recent experience with the property type in the subject property's market. On a practical basis, the appraiser rarely produces a quantity survey method independently. Frequently, the appraiser will receive a set of plans along with a contractor's estimate of construction costs for new construction, and the appraiser will seek to establish the reliability of the cost estimates by conducting an independent comparative-unit or unit-in-place method analysis. Once this verification process has been completed, the appraiser will include the contractor's cost estimates in the appraisal report as well as his or her own independent cost estimates so that the reader can assess the reliability of construction cost estimates. An example of the quantity survey method is not provided in this section.

Reconciliation of the Reproduction Cost New

Using both comparative-unit methods and the unit-in-place method, the following estimates are provided:

Comparative-unit method (primary data):	$4,815,000
Comparative-unit method (secondary data):	$4,800,000
Unit-in-place method (secondary data):	$4,600,000

At this point, the appraiser would evaluate the reliability of the data and techniques and conclude a final estimate of the reproduction cost new of the subject office building. For discussion purposes, $4,800,000 will be used as a reliable estimate of the reproduction cost.

Exhibit 7.7 provides an outline of the cost approach inputs that includes the land value and reproduction cost estimates derived so far.

Step 3. Depreciation

After estimating the reproduction cost new, the appraiser estimates and deducts depreciation to arrive at a depreciated cost new of the building improvements. The term *depreciation* as used here is much different

Exhibit 7.7 Outline of the Cost Approach

Reproduction cost	$4,800,000	
Depreciation		
Physical deterioration:		
Curable (deferred maintenance)	$______	
Incurable (short-lived components)	$______	
Incurable (long-lived components)	$______	
Total physical deterioration		– $______
Functional obsolescence:		
Functional curable	$______	
Functional incurable (superadequacy)	$______	
Total functional obsolescence		– $______
Economic obsolescence		– $______
Total depreciation	– $______	
Depreciated value of building improvements		$______
Depreciated value of site improvements		$______
Land value		$ 650,000
Total		$______
Rounded		$______

than the depreciation referred to in the tax code. In this discussion, depreciation is the difference between the reproduction cost of the building and its current market value, whereas the depreciation cited in the tax code is a function of a legislative ruling that is required for taxation purposes. Depreciation, as used for the purposes of this discussion, can result from three types of sources.

- Physical deterioration
- Functional obsolescence
- External obsolescence

These sources are also known as elements of depreciation.

Physical deterioration is loss in value caused by wear, tear, age, and use. Building improvements begin to experience physical deterioration immediately after construction. The rate of physical deterioration depends on the quality of construction and the level of maintenance. Well-maintained office buildings have less depreciation from physical deterioration as compared to office buildings that are poorly maintained.

Functional obsolescence results from deficiencies or superadequacies in the structure. Essentially, functional obsolescence is a result of a design flaw or a change in tastes and preferences that result in an inferior design as compared to contemporary standards. Functional obsolescence is frequently found in older buildings that are outdated or unable to accommodate modern technology, such as high-speed Internet or other communication technologies.

External obsolescence is a defect caused by negative influences outside a site and is generally incurable on the part of the owner, landlord, or tenant. This form of obsolescence is aptly named because the decline in value occurs from something off-site. Examples include a nearby dairy farm that generates noxious odors or a severely oversupplied office market that has resulted in a decline in rental and occupancy rates. This latter type of obsolescence is sometimes referred to as *economic obsolescence* because the decline in property value results from an economic anomaly.

Estimating Depreciation

The three methods for estimating depreciation are

1. The economic age-life method
2. The extraction method
3. The breakdown method

These methods have been placed in ascending order of complexity and frequency of use. The age-life method estimates depreciation by dividing the effective age by the economic life of the improvements. *Effective age* is property age that is based on the amount of observed deterioration and obsolescence it has sustained; this may be different from its chronological age.

The estimate of effective age is subjectively derived by the appraiser after carefully inspecting the property and assessing market conditions. If a property has been well maintained and is functionally designed and the market is economically sound, the effective age may be less than the actual age. However, if the property has been poorly maintained and is poorly designed and/or the market conditions are depressed, the effective age may be greater than the actual age. This is clearly a call by the appraiser based on empirical evidence and sound reasoning.

Economic life is the period over which improvements to real property contribute to property value. Economic life is an estimate that is generally not determined by the appraiser but instead derived from general estimates of economic life for comparable buildings in the same area. A number of cost-estimating firms track demolitions of various property types and then compile estimates of typical economic lives; these firms are an excellent resource for estimates of economic life. The difference between the effective age of a building and its economic life results in an estimate of the remaining economic life of the building. As noted previously, the effective age divided by the economic life results in an estimate of total depreciation.

Market Extraction Method

In the market extraction method, the appraiser extracts depreciation from comparable sales in a multistep process. First, land value is estimated and deducted from each comparable sale, resulting in the improvement value. Second, the reproduction cost of the building improvements is estimated. Third, the adjusted sale price (deduction for land value) is deducted from the cost new to provide a dollar estimate of depreciation from all forms. This estimate is then divided by the cost new to arrive at a lump-sum percentage in depreciation.

Breakdown Method

The breakdown method is significantly more complex than the market extraction method or estimating depreciation. The breakdown method very precisely estimates each of the three forms of depreciation: physical deterioration, functional obsolescence, and external obsolescence. In practice, appraisers rarely estimate depreciation using this method because of its complexity and arduous data requirements. The following is an example of the breakdown method.

Breakdown Method Example

Curable Physical Deterioration

After inspecting the Maple Landing office building, the appraiser identifies four items which require immediate attention.

1. Sheet rock supporting door stopper in men's restroom is damaged.
2. Sheet rock on exterior canopy is cracked and damaged.
3. Some interior offices need painting.
4. Carpets need cleaning.

Depreciation for these items is considered the cost of restoring the item to new or "like new" condition. The cost of restoring or fixing these items is estimated as follows:

1. Broken sheet rock (men's restroom)	$200
2. Broken sheet rock (exterior canopy)	600
3. Painting	2,250
4. Carpet cleaning	1,900
Total curable physical deterioration	$4,950

Incurable Physical Deterioration

Incurable physical deterioration is measured by separately analyzing the short-lived and long-lived building components. A *short-lived item* is a building component with an expected remaining economic life that is shorter than the remaining economic life of the entire structure. A *long-lived item* is a building component with an expected remaining economic life that is the same as the remaining economic life of the entire structure.

Exhibit 7.8 illustrates those items which the appraiser considers to have economic lives that are shorter than the remaining economic life of the entire structure. Estimates of depreciation are also provided for each of the components.

Exhibit 7.8 **Depreciation of Short-Lived Items**

	Reproduction Cost	Effective Age	Useful Life	Depreciation In Percent	Depreciation In Dollars
Carpet	$119,000	2.0 years	6 yrs.	33.0%	$39,270
Floor tile	$12,750	2.0 years	8 yrs.	25.0%	$3,188
HVAC	$146,616*	1.5 years	12 yrs.	12.5%	$18,327
Roof cover	$49,306†	1.5 years	10 yrs.	15.0%	$7,395
Plumbing fixtures	$28,800	1.5 years	35 yrs.	4.3%	$1,239
Electrical fixtures	$37,153	1.5 years	15 yrs.	10.0%	$3,715
Painting (interior offices)	$12,750‡	2.0 years	5 yrs.	40.0%	$5,100
Total incurable physical deterioration, short-lived components	$406,375				$78,234

* Approximately $146,616 of the current reproduction cost of the entire HVAC system is considered short-lived

† Considered adequate to reseal entire roof system for an extended period of time

‡ $2,550 of the current reproduction cost of $15,300 was cured in physical curable, leaving a remainder of $12,750

The incurable physical deterioration on the long-lived components is estimated as

Reproduction cost		$4,800,000
Less reproduction cost of curable		
Physical (deferred maintenance)	$4,950	
Incurable physical (short-lived)	406,375	
		– 411,325
Total long-lived		$4,388,675
Effective age (15 yrs.)	15 years	
Economic life (new–50 yrs.)	50 years	
		× 0.3
Total incurable physical deterioration, long-lived components		$1,316,603

Functional Obsolescence

An important distinction between *functional obsolescence* and *external obsolescence* is that functional obsolescence refers to a defect originating from inside the property while external obsolescence refers to a defect with origins outside the property. Because the defect is within the property for functional obsolescence, it can always be "fixed," although it may not be financially feasible to do so. In other words, the cost to fix the defect may exceed any marginal increase in value. Therefore, functional obsolescence is curable if the marginal increase in value is greater than or equal to the cost to cure. Conversely, functional obsolescence is incurable if the marginal increase in value is less than the cost to cure. Outlining all the types of functional obsolescence and the related methodologies for estimating accrued depreciation is beyond the scope of this book. If the subject property exhibits complex functional obsolescence issues, the appraiser is encouraged to reference *The Appraisal of Real Estate*, 13th edition, for further explanation.

If the subject property has an outdated or unique design that is not well received in the market, there is a high probability that the property suffers from functional obsolescence. Careful examination of this issue is required. The case study property suffers no functional obsolescence, so no deduction is warranted for this item.

External Obsolescence

The formal definition of *external obsolescence* cited previously provides key words that are critical for understanding and correctly analyzing this term. The first key word is *outside*. External obsolescence is effectively a change in property value that results from a factor or factors outside the property. The term *obsolescence* implies a decline in property value that results from outside the property, but this is not always accurate. In fact, sometimes the change in property value can be positive. In both cases, the change in property value is outside the control of the property owner; therefore, if the change is negative, the external obsolescence is incurable.

External obsolescence may result from changes in both physical and economic conditions outside the property. Typically, the appraiser is able to discover and identify these possible sources of external obsolescence by completing a thorough area, neighborhood, and market analysis.

Unlike physical deterioration and functional obsolescence, external obsolescence impacts both land value and improvement value. When estimating external obsolescence, the appraiser must therefore properly allocate the impact to the building improvements because the impact on the land value should have already been captured in the site valuation.

The three primary methods for calculating external obsolescence are

1. Market extraction
2. Capitalization of income loss if the loss is permanent
3. Discount of income loss if the loss is temporary

Market extraction is effectively paired sales analysis wherein the appraiser identifies transactions of similar properties that have one distinct difference: some are impacted by the economic obsolescence, and others are not. The difference in transactions prices may be attributed to the external obsolescence and correctly applied to the subject property.

For income-producing office properties, the external obsolescence influences the net operating income. In this situation, the appraiser must determine if the change in income is permanent or temporary. If the change is permanent, the appraiser may capitalize the change in income to calculate the amount of external obsolescence. If the change is temporary, the appraiser should discount the change by an appropriate rate over the interim period. In all cases, the appraiser must be careful to appropriately allocate the estimate of external obsolescence to the subject improvements. An example of measuring temporary external obsolescence is provided here.

Temporary External Obsolescence Example (Hypothetical Property)

A temporarily overbuilt office market has resulted in declines in rent and increases in vacancy. Prior to the rent decline, the net operating income for the office property was $1,102,000. However, after the decline, the net operating income was $970,000. The decline in income is expected to last three years. A market discount rate for this property type is 12%, and the allocation to the improvements is estimated at 75%. The amount of external obsolescence resulting from the temporarily overbuilt market is calculated in the following three steps.

1. Calculate the net income difference.

$$\$1{,}102{,}000 - \$970{,}000 = \$132{,}000$$

2. Discount the difference over the interim period at the appropriate discount rate. The present value annuity factor for three years at 12% is 2.40183.

$$\$132{,}000 \times 2.40183 = \$317{,}042$$

3. Appropriately allocate the value change to the building improvements.

$$\$317{,}042 \times 0.75 = \$237{,}782$$

Therefore, the depreciation allocated to external obsolescence is $237,782.

This example has been provided for instruction purposes. The Maple Landing property is not impacted by external obsolescence, so no deduction is made for this item.

Step 4. Subtract Total Depreciation from Building Improvements

Total depreciation is subtracted from the reproduction cost of the building improvements to arrive at an estimate of the depreciated cost of the building improvements. Exhibit 7.9 provides a summary of the estimates so far.

Step 5. Estimate and Add the Depreciated Cost New of the Site Improvements

Because of the large contribution to overall value, estimating the depreciated cost of the building improvements has been the primary focus up to this point. Estimating the depreciated cost of the site improvements is the next step in the analysis. Site improvements to office properties frequently include driveways, curbs, gutters, sidewalks, lighting, parking, and landscaping. The procedure for estimating the depreciated cost of the site improvements is similar to building improvements. An example is provided in Exhibit 7.10.

Exhibit 7.9 Outline of the Cost Approach

Reproduction cost		$4,800,000
Depreciation		
Physical deterioration:		
Curable (deferred maintenance)	$4,950	
Incurable (short-lived components)	78,234	
Incurable (long-lived components)	1,316,603	
Total physical deterioration		$1,399,787
Functional obsolescence:		
Functional curable	0	
Functional incurable (superadequacy)	0	
Total functional obsolescence		0
Economic obsolescence		0
Total depreciation		– 1,399,787
Depreciated value of building improvements		$3,400,213
Depreciated value of site improvements		$______
Land value		$650,000
Total		$______
Rounded		$______

Exhibit 7.10 Depreciated Value of Site Improvements

				Depreciation	
	Reproduction Cost	Effective Age	Useful Life	In Percent	In Dollars
Landscaping	$25,355	1.5 yrs.	10 yrs.	15.0	$3,803
Paving	$115,613	1.5 yrs.	10 yrs.	15.0	$17,342
Block wall	$6,960	1.5 yrs.	30 yrs.	5.0	$348
Sidewalk and curbs	$11,399	1.5 yrs.	25 yrs.	6.0	$684
	$159,327				
Total physical deterioration					$22,177

Therefore, the depreciated value of the site improvements is calculated as:

Cost new	$159,327
Less depreciation	– 22,177
	$137,150

Step 6. Conclusion of Value

The final step is primarily a summation process of combining the depreciated cost of the building and site improvements with the site value in its highest and best use. An example of this process is shown in Exhibit 7.11.

Because the cost approach is primarily a summation process, the reconciliation takes place as each step is performed. For instance, multiple methods such as age-life and extraction may have been employed when estimating accrued depreciation. The appraiser assesses the data and reliability of the respective techniques and then selects the most reliable estimate or estimates. This process is effectively duplicated within each of the steps of the cost approach. As a result, the final summation results in the appraiser's best estimate of value via the cost approach.

Exhibit 7.11 Conclusion of Value from the Cost Approach

Reproduction cost		$4,800,000
Depreciation		
Physical deterioration:		
Curable (deferred maintenance)	$4,950	
Incurable (short-lived components)	$78,234	
Incurable (long-lived components)	$1,316,603	
Total physical deterioration		$1,399,787
Functional obsolescence:		
Functional curable	0	
Functional incurable (superadequacy)	0	
Total functional obsolescence		0
Economic obsolescence		0
Total depreciation		– $1,399,787
Depreciated value of building improvements		$3,400,213
Depreciated value of site improvements		137,150
Land value		+ 650,000
Total		$4,187,363
Rounded		$4,200,000

Alternative Valuation Scenarios

As noted in the definition of the cost approach provided at the beginning of this chapter, the cost approach derives a value indication of the fee simple interest in the property. In addition, if the full allocation of entrepreneurial profit is included in the calculation, the value estimate assumes stabilized occupancy. In other words, entrepreneurial profit can be thought of as coming from two sources.

1. An allocation for coordinating the development of the project

2. An allocation for coordinating the absorption of the property to achieve stabilized occupancy

It is incumbent upon the appraiser to obtain an estimate of entrepreneurial profit from the market and to understand its composition. If the estimate of entrepreneurial profit includes both allocations and if a property is being appraised when complete, the appraiser must include a deduction for any costs incurred to achieve stabilized occupancy. These costs typically include leasing commissions and tenant improvements and are deducted as an indirect cost to result in the market value of the fee simple interest when complete.

If the client requests the market value of the leased fee interest from the cost approach, a separate lump sum would have to be added or subtracted as a property rights adjustment. Techniques for estimating the value differential between the leased fee and fee simple interest were provided in the other two approaches to value.

Chapter 8

Reconciliation

In a perfectly efficient market with full transparency of data, applying the three approaches to value–the income capitalization approach, the sales comparison approach, and the cost approach–would theoretically result in the same estimate of value. However, because commercial markets typically suffer from inefficiencies caused by the lack of complete and transparent data, the three approaches to value typically do not result in the same single estimate of value. Furthermore, while appraisers recognize that there is a relevant range of value and would prefer to provide clients with a range rather than a point estimate, clients generally expect a single estimate of value. In any case, the reconciliation process is an important aspect of the appraisal. According to the fourth edition of *The Dictionary of Real Estate Appraisal*, *reconciliation* is the last phase of any valuation assignment, when two or more value indications derived from market data are resolved into a final value opinion that may be either a final range of value or a single point estimate.

In other words, reconciliation is the process of evaluating the respective value conclusions derived from the different methodologies and then concluding to a final opinion of value. The reconciliation process essentially requires a re-examination of specific data, procedures, and techniques used to derive the alternative value estimates. Each valuation method or approach is reviewed and compared to the other approaches in terms of adequacy and reliability of data, soundness of analysis, and reliance placed on that method by market participants. It is imperative that the appraiser carefully consider and appropriately weight methodologies used most frequently by market participants as he or she concludes to a final opinion of value. It is also essential that the reconciliation be made in the context of the definition of value (as cited in the report), property rights appraised, property occupancy assumptions, effective date of valuation, and any assumptions or limiting conditions.

Review

The reconciliation begins with a comprehensive review of all the data and analysis used in the appraisal process. This includes a careful examination of the data (reliability and adequacy) and a verification of the accuracy of all adjustments and calculations. A careful review and consideration of the appropriateness of the valuation methodologies should also be considered.

Cautions

When value estimates differ, the appraiser should be inquisitive and strive to understand and explain these differences. This process leads to greater insight into the nuances of the subject property's market and is greatly appreciated by the readers of the report. Each valuation approach exhibits strengths and weaknesses depending on the characteristics and attributes of the subject property and market conditions. It is important that the appraiser educate the reader by discussing these strengths and weaknesses in the context of the subject property's appraisal. For instance, the appraiser might note that the income capitalization approach is given more reliance for large multitenant office properties in the subject's market. As a result, more weight would be given to this approach in the final valuation. Conversely, the appraiser might note that the cost approach is given less weight when the property is older and suffers from many forms of accrued depreciation. In short, a careful discussion of the strengths and weaknesses of each approach to value provides the reasoning that leads the reader of the report to the same conclusion reached by the appraiser. This, in turn, addresses the criticisms often leveled at appraisers for providing "believe me because I said it" conclusions.

The appraiser should be careful about using an equation or formula, such as an arithmetic mean, to arrive at a conclusion during the reconciliation process. An equation- or formula-based conclusion typically implies a level of precision in the valuation process that may not exist. In addition, these measures are often inferior to the sound judgment of an experienced appraiser.

Glossary

AAA tenant. A tenant who has a very good (AAA) credit rating according to a recognized rating bureau; also called *prime tenant* or *creditworthy tenant.*[1]

absolute net lease. A lease in which the tenant pays all expenses including structural maintenance and repairs; usually a long-term lease to a credit tenant.

average daily traffic (ADT). The average traffic volume measured at a selected highway location on a single day; the sum of all traffic recorded for a given period of time divided by the number of days in that period.

back office. The internal operations of an organization that are not accessible or visible to the general public. Back-office space does not require the same level of finish as Class A office space.

base rent. The minimum rent stipulated in a lease.

BOMA standard. The standard method of floor measurement for office buildings as defined by the Building Owners and Managers Association.

build-out. Interior construction that converts raw space into finished space ready for occupancy; includes installation of equipment, finish carpentry, construction of amenities, and initial tenant improvements.

business park. A master-planned development encompassing a group of industrial and/or office buildings on a large acreage tract with wide streets. Higher quality parks will feature a campus-like setting with extensive landscaping, underground utilities, high architectural standards, and conditions, covenants, and restrictions (CC&Rs) to promote a harmonious and attractive working environment.

---

1. Unless otherwise noted, all definitions are taken from *The Dictionary of Real Estate Appraisal*, 4th ed. (Chicago: Appraisal Institute, 2002).

capital expenditure. Investments of cash or the creation of liability to acquire or improve an asset, e.g., land, buildings, building additions, site improvements, machinery, equipment; as distinguished from cash outflows for expense items that are normally considered part of the current period's operations.

capture rate. The estimated percentage of the total potential market for a specific type of property, e.g., office space, retail space, single-family homes, that is currently absorbed by existing facilities or is forecast to be absorbed by proposed facilities. For example, the capture rate of a retail center depends on the size of its trade area, the anchor tenants in the facility, competition within the trade area, and the relative position of the subject facility compared to the competition. Short-term capture is referred to as *absorption*; long-term capture is referred to as *share of the market.*

central business district (CBD). The core, or downtown area, of a city where the major retail, financial, governmental, professional, recreational, and service activities of the community are concentrated. *See also* **uptown.**

central city. The primary city in a standard metropolitan area, from which the name of the area is usually taken. *See also* **metropolitan statistical area (MSA).**

circulation pattern. The traffic pattern established in moving from one place to another on foot or by car, e.g., from home to business, to or past a specific location.

class of construction. Buildings are divided into five basic cost groups by type of frame (supporting columns and beams), floor, roof, and walls.

- **Class A construction.** Frame is structural steel columns and beams, fireproofed with masonry, concrete, plaster, or other noncombustible material. Floors are concrete or concrete on steel deck, and fireproofed. Roof is formed concrete, precast slabs, concrete or gypsum on steel deck, and fireproofed. Walls are non-bearing curtain walls, masonry, concrete, metal and glass panels, stone, steel studs and masonry, tile, or stucco, etc.
- **Class B construction.** Frame is reinforced concrete columns and beams, and of fire-resistant construction. Floors are concrete or concrete on steel deck, and fireproofed. Roof is formed concrete, precast slabs, concrete, or gypsum on steel deck, and fireproofed. Walls are non-bearing curtain walls, masonry, concrete, metal and glass panels, stone, steel studs and masonry, tile, or stucco, etc.

- **Class C construction.** Frame is masonry or concrete load-bearing walls with or without pilasters. Masonry, concrete or curtain walls with full or partial open steel, wood, or concrete frame. Floors are wood or concrete plank on wood or steel floor joists, or concrete slab on grade. Roof is wood or steel joists with wood or steel deck, or concrete plank. Walls are brick, concrete block, or tile masonry, tilt-up, formed concrete, non-bearing curtain walls.
- **Class D construction.** Frame is wood or steel studs in bearing wall, full or partial open wood or steel frame, and primarily combustible construction. Floors are wood or steel floor joists, or concrete slab on grade. Roof is wood or steel joists with wood, or steel deck. Walls are almost any material except bearing or curtain walls of solid masonry or concrete, and generally combustible construction.
- **Class S construction.** Frame is metal bents, columns, girders, purlins, and girts without fireproofing, and of incombustible construction. Floors are wood or steel deck on steel floor joists, or concrete slab on grade. Roof is steel or wood deck on steel joists. Walls are metal skin or sandwich panels, and generally incombustible (i.e., pre-manufactured metal construction). (Marshall & Swift)

class of office building. For the purposes of comparison, office space is grouped into three classes. These classes represent a subjective quality rating of buildings, which indicates the competitive ability of each building to attract similar types of tenants. Combinations of factors such as rent, building finishes, system standards and efficiency, building amenities, location/accessibility, and market perception are used as relative measures. (Note that national cost estimating services may classify office buildings differently than local markets.)

- **Class A** office buildings are the most prestigious office buildings competing for the premier office users, with rents above average for the area. Buildings have high-quality standard finishes, state-of-the-art systems, exceptional accessibility, and a definite market presence.
- **Class B** office buildings compete for a wide range of users, with rents in the average range for the area. Building finishes are fair to good for the area and systems are adequate, but the buildings do not compete with Class A buildings at the same price.
- **Class C** office buildings compete for tenants requiring functional space at rents below the average for the area.

commercial condominium. The application of the condominium concept to commercial, industrial, or office space.

common area. The total area within a property that is not designed for sale or rental but is available for common use by all owners, tenants, or their invitees, e.g., parking and its appurtenances, malls, sidewalks, landscaped areas, recreation areas, public toilets, truck and service facilities.

common area maintenance (CAM). The expense of operating and maintaining common areas; may or may not include management charges and usually does not include capital expenditures on tenant improvements or other improvements to the property. *See also* **common area.**

condominium. A multiunit structure or property in which persons hold fee simple title to individual units and an undivided interest in common areas.

demising partition. A physical barrier that designates a tenant space or establishes a leasable area and separates it from the remaining space; may be a limited common element as part of an undivided ownership interest in a condominium development. Condominium ownership is based on the area from the demising wall surface to the facing wall surface.

economic rent. In appraisal, a term sometimes used as a synonym for market rent.

effective rent. The rental rate net of financial concessions such as periods of no rent during the lease term; may be calculated on a discounted basis, reflecting the time value of money, or on a simple, straight-line basis.

efficiency ratio. In appraising, the ratio between the net rentable area of a building, i.e., the space used and occupied exclusively by tenants, and its gross area, which includes the building's core.

escalation clause. A clause in an agreement that provides for the adjustment of a price or rent based on some event or index, e.g., a provision to increase rent if operating expenses increase; also called *expense recovery clause.*

escalator lease. A lease that requires the lessor to pay expenses for the first year and the lessee to pay any necessary increases in expenses as additional rent over the subsequent years of the lease.

excess rent. The amount by which contract rent exceeds market rent at the time of the appraisal; created by a lease favorable to the landlord (lessor) and may reflect a locational advantage, unusual management, unknowledgeable parties, or a lease execution in an earlier, stronger rental market. Due to the higher risk inherent in the receipt of excess rent, it may be calculated separately and capitalized at a higher rate in the income capitalization approach.

expense stop. A clause in a lease that limits the landlord's expense obligation because the lessee assumes any expenses above an established level.

flat rental lease. A lease with a specified level of rent that continues throughout the lease term; also called *level payment lease.*

flex space. Industrial space designed to allow flexible conversion of warehouse or manufacturing space to a higher percentage of office space. Alternatively known as a *service center* or *tech space.*

floor area. The total horizontal surface of a specific floor; the total area of all floors in a multistory building, computed from the outside building walls of each floor with balcony and mezzanine areas computed separately and added to the total.

floor area ratio (FAR). The relationship between the above-ground floor area of a building, as described by the building code, and the area of the plot on which it stands; in planning and zoning, often expressed as a decimal, e.g., a ratio of 2.0 indicates that the permissible floor area of a building is twice the total land area. *See also* **land-to-building ratio.**

freestanding building. A building that is not attached to another building.

frictional vacancy. Vacancy unrelated to disequilibria in supply and demand, but rather due to tenant relocations as leases roll over and expire. Frictional vacancy is considered a typical vacancy rate in a given market operating in equilibrium. Typically used in demographic analysis or supply and demand studies. Closely related but distinct from the concept of vacancy and collection loss as it relates to a single property.

general vacancy. A method of calculating any remaining vacancy and collection loss considerations when using discounted cash flow (DCF) analysis, where turnover vacancy has been used as part of the income estimate. The combined effects of turnover vacancy and general vacancy relate to total vacancy and collection loss. *See also* **turnover vacancy.**

graduated rental lease. A lease that provides for specified changes in rent at one or more points during the lease term; e.g., step-up and step-down leases.

gross area

1. The total area of a structure without deducting for holes or cutouts.
2. The entire area of a roof.
3. In construction, the entire area of a shingle, including any parts that might have had to be cut out.
4. The total enclosed floor area of a building. (R.S. Means)

gross building area (GBA). The total floor area of a building, including below-grade space but excluding unenclosed areas, measured from the exterior of the walls. Gross building area for office buildings is computed by measuring to the outside finished surface of permanent outer building walls without any deductions. All enclosed floors of the building including basements, mechanical equipment floors, penthouses, and the like are included in the measurement. Parking spaces and parking garages are excluded.

gross floor area. The total area of all the floors of a building, including intermediately floored tiers, mezzanine, basements, etc., as measured from the exterior surfaces of the outside walls of the building. (R.S. Means)

gross lease. A lease in which the landlord receives stipulated rent and is obligated to pay all or most of the property's operating expenses and real estate taxes.

gross up method. A method of calculating variable operating expenses in income-producing properties when less than 100% occupancy is assumed. The gross up method approximates the actual expense of providing services to the rentable area of a building given a specified rate of occupancy.

gross rental basis. Refers to a lease that stipulates that the lessor pays all operating expenses of the real estate.

high rise

1. An indefinite term for a multistory building that is serviced by elevators.
2. A building with upper floors higher than fire department aerial ladders, usually ten or more stories. (R.S. Means)

high-rise office building. A multistory office building, usually having 25 floors or more.

holdover tenant. A tenant who remains in possession of the leased real estate after the lease has expired; in many states the lease is automatically renewed if the lessor accepts a rent payment after the expiration of the lease. The rental rate during the holdover period is often 150% of the prior monthly rental rate as incentive for the tenant to renegotiate the lease or vacate.

index lease. A lease, usually for a long term, that provides for periodic rent adjustments based on the change in an economic index, e.g., a cost-of-living index.

institutional property. Property of a public nature owned and operated by the government or by a nonprofit organization; e.g., hospitals, orphanages, private and public educational facilities, correctional facilities, museums; also certain private properties, e.g., banks, insurance companies.

land-to-building ratio. The proportion of land area to gross building area; one of the factors determining comparability of properties. *See also* **floor area ratio (FAR).**

lease rollover. The expiration of a lease and the subsequent re-leasing of the space.

leasing commissions. Fees paid to an agent for leasing tenant space. When leasing fees are spread over the term of a lease or lease renewal, they are treated as a variable operating expense. Initial leasing fees usually fall under capital expenditures for development and are not included among periodic expenses.

local economic analysis. Study of the fundamental determinants of the demand for and supply of all real estate in the market. The analysis considers the factors basic to the demand for all types of real estate in a local economy–i.e., population, households, employment, and income. Past trends and forecasts of these basic demand determinants are made for a defined geographic area. The supply-side factors to be considered include the amount of land available for specific land uses, construction costs, and the local infrastructure. Economic base analysis and input-output analysis are two techniques used to describe the local economy.

management fee. An expense item representing the sum paid or the value of management service; a variable operating expense, usually expressed as a percentage of effective gross income.

market rent. The most probable rent that a property should bring in a competitive and open market reflecting all conditions and restrictions of the typical lease agreement, including the rental adjustment and revaluation, permitted uses, use restrictions, expense obligations, term, concessions, renewal and purchase options, and tenant improvements (TIs). (*The Appraisal of Real Estate*, 13th ed.)

medical center. A large medical complex that provides a comprehensive array of health care services in both outpatient and inpatient settings.

medical office. A building containing space designated for medical functions such as doctors, dentistry, medical lab, or medical facilities. The space is typically air-conditioned and specially finished for medical functions in terms of providing a greater number of wall subdivisions for treatment rooms and additional plumbing. Medical uses are typically parking-intensive with standard parking requirements of five spaces per 1,000 square feet.

metropolitan statistical area (MSA). A city of at least 50,000 people; an urbanized area of at least 50,000 with a total metropolitan population of at least 100,000; designated under standards set in 1980 by the Federal Committee on MSAs. This term replaces the term *standard metropolitan statistical area (SMSA).*

net effective rent. Rental rate adjusted for lease concessions.

net lease. Generally a lease in which the tenant pays for utilities, janitorial services, and either property taxes or insurance, and the landlord pays for maintenance, repairs, and the property taxes or insurance not paid by the tenant. Also called *single net lease*, *modified gross lease*, and *semi-gross lease*; sometimes used synonymously with *single net lease* but better stated as a *partial net lease* to eliminate confusion.

net net lease. Generally a lease in which the tenant pays for utilities, janitorial services, property taxes, and insurance in addition to the rent, and the landlord pays for maintenance and repairs. Also called *double net lease*, *NN*, *modified gross lease*, and *semi-gross lease*; sometimes used synonymously with *single net lease* but better stated as a *partial net lease* to eliminate confusion.

net net net lease. A net lease under which the lessee assumes all expenses of operating a property, including both fixed and variable expenses and any common area maintenance that might apply, but the landlord is responsible for structural repairs. Also called *triple net lease* or *NNN* but better stated as a *fully net lease*.

office-hotel. An office property designed for timesharing. Shared amenities include meeting/board rooms with state-of-the-art teleconferencing; central telephone systems; business support technologies; access to online data services; on-demand temporary offices and personnel; courier services; concierge services to arrange travel, hotel, car, restaurant, and theater reservations; discounts on furniture and office equipment; child care centers; and fitness and catering facilities. The amenities generate income to landlords while supporting the alternative office strategies of tenants. Payment for such services are either incorporated into the lease or charged on a per-use basis.

office park. A business park dominated by office uses; may be designed to appeal to a certain type of tenant (e.g., medical facilities, research facilities); often contains more office support facilities (restaurants, other retail) than an industrial park and typically does not allow intensive industrial uses.

office/showroom. Similar to flex/office space in terms of basic construction and layout with 50% of the interior finished and above-standard parking (3:1). Office/showrooms are typically located along freeways or major thoroughfares where traffic exposure can be exploited for the purpose of retail/direct sales. Interior build-out typically favors a sales floor over office space with the balance of space devoted to warehouse/stock.

overage rent. The percentage rent paid over and above the guaranteed minimum rent or base rent; calculated as a percentage of sales in excess of a specified breakeven sales volume.

owner-occupied. Describes real estate physically occupied by the owner as opposed to property owned by an investor or absentee landlord and rented to tenants. An owner-occupant can usually obtain better mortgage rates and preferred tax treatment.

parking ratio. The number of available parking spaces per rentable unit of area, residential unit, hotel room, restaurant seat, etc.; also, the ratio of total parking area to gross leasable area. The parking ratio is a standard comparison that indicates the relationship between parking spaces or parking area and an economic or physical unit of comparison.

percentage lease. A lease in which the rent or some portion of the rent represents a specified percentage of the volume of business, productivity, or use achieved by the tenant.

property management. The process of maintaining and creating value in real property consistent with the owner's objectives and in compliance with the highest standard of professional ethics. In real estate, the process of profitable operation and management of owned, leased, or subleased real property for a building owner, developer, or landlord. (Building Owners and Managers Institute International (BOMI))

renewal option. The right, but not the obligation, of a tenant to continue a lease at a specified term and rent.

rentable area. The amount of space on which the rent is based; calculated according to local practice.

rent concession. A discount or other benefit offered by a landlord to induce a prospective tenant to enter into a lease; usually in the form of one or more months of free rent, but it may be expressed in extra services to the tenant or some other consideration; also called *rent offset.*

rent control. A legal regulation that specifies the maximum rental payment for the use of property.

rent loss insurance. Insurance that protects a landlord against loss of rent or rental value due to fire or other casualty that renders the leased premises unavailable for use and as a result of which the tenant is excused from paying rent.

rent-up period. A period of time during which a rental property is in the process of initial leasing; may begin before or after construction and lasts until stabilized occupancy is achieved.

replacement allowance. An allowance that provides for the periodic replacement of building components that wear out more rapidly than the building itself and must be replaced during the building's economic life.

revaluation lease. A lease that provides for periodic rent adjustments based on a revaluation of the real estate under prevailing market rental conditions.

sandwich lease. A lease in which an intermediate, or sandwich, leaseholder is the lessee of one party and the lessor of another. The owner of the sandwich lease is neither the fee owner nor the user of the property; he or she may be a leaseholder in a chain of leases, excluding the ultimate sublessee.

scheduled rent. Income due under existing leases.

stabilized income. Income at that point in time when abnormalities in supply and demand or any additional transitory conditions cease to exist and the existing conditions are those expected to continue over the economic life of the property; projected income that is subject to change, but has been adjusted to reflect an equivalent, stable annual income. *See also* **stabilized occupancy.**

stabilized occupancy. Occupancy at that point in time when abnormalities in supply and demand or any additional transitory conditions cease to exist and the existing conditions are those expected to continue over the economic life of the property; the optimum range of long-term occupancy that an income-producing real estate project is expected to achieve under competent management after exposure for leasing in the open market for a reasonable period of time at terms and conditions comparable to competitive offerings. *See also* **stabilized income.**

sublease. An agreement in which the lessee in a prior lease conveys the right of use and occupancy of a property to another, the sublessee for a specific period of time, which may or may not be coterminous with the underlying lease term.

submarket. A division of a total market that reflects the preferences of a particular set of buyers and sellers.

tenant improvement allowance. A dollar amount provided to the tenant by the landlord for the construction of tenant improvements, which may or may not equal the cost of construction or remodeling.

traffic survey. A survey conducted to obtain traffic information, e.g., data on traffic quantity and composition, travelers' origins and destinations, the purpose of trips, means of transportation; usually related to a specific time on a certain day of the week.

turnover vacancy. A method of calculating vacancy allowance that is estimated or considered as part of the potential income estimate when using discounted cash flow (DCF) analysis. As units or suites turn over and are available for re-leasing, the periodic vacancy time frame (vacancy window) to re-lease the space is considered. Accordingly the income estimate reflects a component of vacancy and is not true potential gross income but some level of effective gross income. *See also* **general vacancy.**

uptown. A business district developed to relieve congestion in the central business district, generally along a major arterial providing access to the suburbs. *See also* **central business district (CBD).**

usable area. The area available for assignment or rental to an occupant, including every type of usable space; measured from the inside finish of outer walls to the office side of corridors or permanent partitions and from the centerline of adjacent spaces; includes subdivided occupant space, but no deductions are made for columns and projections. There are two variations of net area: single occupant net assignable area and store net assignable area.

vacancy and collection loss. A deduction from potential gross income (*PGI*) made to reflect income reductions due to vacancies, tenant turnover, and nonpayment of rent; also called *vacancy and credit loss* or *vacancy and contingency loss.* Often it is expressed as a percent of *PGI* and should reflect the competitive market. Its treatment can differ according to the interest being appraised, property type, capitalization method, and whether the property is at stabilized occupancy. (*The Appraisal of Real Estate*, 13th ed.)

vacancy rate.

1. The relationship between the amount of vacant space and total space in a building or market; expressed as a percentage.
2. The relationship between the rent estimated for vacant building space and the total rent estimated for all the space in the building. *See also* **frictional vacancy.**

Bibliography

Chapter 1. The Origin and History of Office Properties

Girouard, Mark. *Cities and People.* New Haven, CT: Yale University Press, 1985.

Goldberger, Paul. *The Skyscraper.* New York: Alfred A. Knopf, 1982.

Lehman, A. "The New York Skyscraper: A History of Its Development, 1870-1939." PhD dissertation, Yale University, 1974.

Mujica, Francisco. *History of the Skyscraper.* New York: DaCapo Press, 1977.

Roth, Leland M. *A Concise History of American Architecture.* New York: Harper & Row, 1979.

Schultz, Earl, and Walter Simmons. *Offices in the Sky.* Indianapolis: Bobbs-Merrill, 1959.

Tallmadge, Thomas Eddy, ed. *The Origin of the Skyscraper.* Chicago: Alderbrink Press, 1939.

Chapter 2. Types of Office Buildings and Valuation Nuances

Bell, Randall. "Medical Office Building Appraisal." *The Appraisal Journal* (April 1995).

Donnelly, J. C. "Investor Attitudes and the Appraisal of the Major Urban Center Office Building." *The Appraisal Journal* (January 1981).

Gimmy, Arthur E. "The Doctor's Office: An Intimate Examination." *The Appraisal Journal* (October 1975).

Healy, M. J. "Valuation of a Distressed Office Building." *The Appraisal Journal* (July 1989): 372-377.

Schafer, Scott M. "Bank Branch Valuation: An Empirical Approach." *The Appraisal Journal* (April 1994).

White, John R. "How to Plan and Build a Major Office Building." *Real Estate Review,* vol. 10, no. 1 (1980): 3-7.

White, John R., ed. *The Office Building: From Concept to Investment Reality.* Chicago: Appraisal Institute, American Society of Real Estate Counselors, and Society of Industrial and Office Realtors, 1993.

Williams, D. L. "Suburban Activity Centers and Corporate Decisions." *Perspective* (a publication of the Society of Industrial and Office Realtors (SIOR)), no. 5 (1985).

Wofford, Larry E. "Significant Trends Affecting Office and Industrial Real Estate: A Twenty-First Century Perspective." *The Appraisal Journal* (January 1987): 94-107.

Chapter 3. Site Analysis

Bible, Douglas S., and Chengho Hsieh. "Determinants of Vacant Land Values and Implications for Appraisers." *The Appraisal Journal* (July 1999): 264-268.

January, David J. "Forecasting Lot Values Using Regression Analysis." *The Real Estate Appraiser and Analyst* (Fall 1989): 61-72.

Rabianski, Joseph S. "Site Size Adjustments: A Technique to Estimate the Adjustment Magnitude." *The Appraisal Journal* (Fall 2005): 397-407.

Rabianski, Joseph S., and S. W. Wright. "Non-Economic Factors in the Site Selection Process." *Real Estate Issues,* vol. 7, no. 2 (Fall/Winter 1982): 25-27.

Waldron, Deloris M. "Analyzing Land Sales: A Case Study." *The Real Estate Appraiser and Analyst* (Fall 1988): 34-40.

Wright, Robert T., and Morton Gitelman. *Land Use in a Nutshell.* St. Paul, MN: West Group, 2000.

Chapter 4. Improvement Analysis

Adler, R. H. "Revisiting the Smart Building Debate." *Professional Report of Industrial and Office Real Estate,* SIOR, July/August 1991.

Alberts, R. J., and T. M. Clauretie. "Commercial Real Estate and the Americans with Disabilities Act: Implications for Appraisers." *The Appraisal Journal* (July 1992): 347-356.

Barlow, Philip. M. "How to Make an Inspection." *The Appraisal Journal* (October 1985).

Colwell, Peter F., and Henry J. Munneke. "Bargaining Strength and Property Class in Office Markets." *The Journal of Real Estate Finance and Economics* (November 2006).

Graham, Marshall. F., and Douglas S. Bible. "Classifications for Commercial Real Estate." *The Appraisal Journal* (April 1992).

Guidry, Krisandra. "Sick Commercial Buildings: What Appraisers Need to Know." *The Appraisal Journal* (January 2002).

Healy, John J., and Patricia Healy. "Lenders' Perspectives on Environmental Issues." *The Appraisal Journal* (October 1992): 394-398.

Kimball, William. J. "Measuring an Office Building: 1 + 1 = 2.2." *The Appraisal Journal* (January 1988).

King, N. S. "Economic Impact of Current Parking Standards on Office Developments." *Real Estate Issues,* vol. 8, no. 2 (Fall/Winter 1983): 49-50.

Miller, Norman G. "Telecommunications Technology and Real Estate: Some Additional Perspectives." *Real Estate Finance* (Summer 1996).

Mundy, Bill. "Defining a Trophy Property." *The Appraisal Journal* (October 2002).

Simpson, John A. *Property Inspection: An Appraiser's Guide.* Chicago: Appraisal Institute, 1997.

Wheaton, William C. "A Perspective on Telecommunications Technology and Real Estate: Office, Industrial, and Retail Markets." *Real Estate Finance* (Summer 1996).

Chapter 5. The Income Capitalization Approach

Market Analysis

Archer, W. R. "Determinants of Location for General-Purpose Office Firms Within Medium-Sized Cities." *Journal of the American Real Estate and Urban Economics Association* (Fall 1981).

Bateman, M. *Office Development: A Geographical Analysis.* New York: St. Martin's Press, 1985.

Bible, Douglas S., and John W. Whaley. "Projecting an Urban Office Market: A Source of Information for Appraisers." *The Appraisal Journal* (October 1983): 515-523.

Birch, D. L. "Forecasting Over-Built Office Markets." *Perspective* (SIOR), no. 20 (1988).

Brueggeman, William B. "The Relative Attraction of CBD Versus Suburban Locations in Major Office Markets." *Real Estate Finance* (Fall 1996): 15-21.

Corcoran, Patrick J. "Searching for the Bottom of the Office Market." *Real Estate Review* (Spring 1993): 15-21.

Fanning, Stephen F. "Existing Office Building." In *Market Analysis for Real Estate: Concepts and Applications in Valuation and Highest and Best Use.* edited by Stephen F. Fanning, 269-306. Chicago: Appraisal Institute, 2005.

Gallagher, Mark, and Antony P. Wood. "Fear of Overbuilding in the Office Sector: How Real is the Risk and Can We Predict It?" *The Journal of Real Estate Research* (1999): 3-32.

Gordon, Jacques, Paige Mosbaugh, and Todd Canter. "Integrating Regional Economic Indicators with the Real Estate Cycle." *The Journal of Real Estate Research* (1996): 469-501.

Hakfoort, Jacco, and Robert Lie. "Office Space per Worker: Evidence from Four European Markets." *The Journal of Real Estate Research* (1996): 183-196.

Hanink, Dean M. "How 'Local' are Local Office Markets?" *Real Estate Economics* (1996): 341-358.

Hinda, D. S., and J. B. Corgel. "Understanding the Effect of Transportation on Office Location." *Perspective*, no. 1 (1984).

Howarth, Robin A., and Emil E. Malizia. "Office Market Analysis: Improving Best-Practice Techniques." *Journal of Real Estate Research* (1998): 15-34.

Howland, Marie, and David S. Wessel. "Projecting Suburban Office Space Demand: Alternative Estimates of Employment in Offices." *The Journal of Real Estate Research* (Summer 1994): 369-389.

Kateley, Richard. "Office Marketability Studies." In *The Office Building: From Concept to Investment Reality*, edited by John Robert White, 184-202. Chicago: Counselors of Real Estate, 1993.

Kimball, J. R., and Barbara S. Bloomberg. "Office Space Demand Analysis." *The Appraisal Journal* (October 1987): 567-577.

Legg, W. E. "Analysis of Office Space Markets." *Perspective*, no. 7 (1988).

Liang, Youguo, and John H. Kim. "Demand for Office Space: Neither Feast nor Famine." *Real Estate Finance* (Summer 1998): 37-44.

Malizia, Emil E., and Robin A. Howarth. "Clarifying the Structure and Advancing the Practice of Real Estate Market Analysis." *The Appraisal Journal* (January 1995): 60-68.

McClure, Kirk. "Estimating Occupied Office Space: Comparing Alternative Forecast Methodologies." *The Journal of Real Estate Research* (Fall 1991): 305-314.

Niedercorn, J. H., and B. V. Bechdolt. "An Economic Derivation of the Gravity Law of Spatial Interaction." *Journal of Regional Science*, vol. 9 (1969): 273-282.

Pearson, T. D. "Location! Location! Location! What is Location?" *The Appraisal Journal* (January 1991): 7-20.

Powers, R. T., and B. F. Hunter. "Anticipating Office and Industrial Space Demand: How to Effectively Anticipate a Market Area's Turning Points." *Perspective*, no. 26 (1989).

Rabianski, Joseph S. "Linking Particular Office Marketability to the Market." *Real Estate Review* (Fall 1994): 83-86.

———. "Market Analyses and Appraisals: Problems Persist." *Real Estate Review* (Winter 1995): 45-49.

———. "Primary and Secondary Data: Concepts, Concerns, Errors, and Issues." *The Appraisal Journal* (January 2003): 43-55.

———. "Vacancy in Market Analysis and Valuation." *The Appraisal Journal* (April 2002): 191-199.

Rabianski, Joseph S., and Karen M. Gibler. "Office Market Demand Analysis and Estimation Techniques: A Literature Review, Synthesis, and Commentary." *Journal of Real Estate Literature* (2007): 37-56.

Rages, W. R., et al. "Forecasting Office Space Demands and Office Space per Worker Estimates." *Perspective*, no. 34 (1992).

Roberts, D. F. *Marketing and Leasing of Office Space.* Chicago: Institute of Real Estate Management, 1986.

Rosen, K. T. "Toward a Model of the Office Building Sector." *Journal of the American Real Estate and Urban Economics Association* (Fall 1984).

Runnels, James A. "Projecting Demand for Office Space in Dallas." *The Appraisal Journal* (January 1986): 118-123.

Shilton, Leon. "The Changing Demand for Office Space." *Real Estate Review* (Summer 1995): 89-94.

Weaver, William C. "Forecasting Office Space Demand with Conjoint Measurement Techniques." *The Appraisal Journal* (July 1984): 389-398.

Wincott, D. Richard, and Glenn R. Mueller. "Market Analysis in the Appraisal Process." *The Appraisal Journal* (January 1995): 27-32.

Wurtzebach, C. H. "Real Estate Feasibility Analysis and the Emerging Public-Private Partnership in Land Use Decisions." *Real Estate Issues*, vol. 6, no. 2 (Fall/Winter 1981): 12-16.

Rent and Vacancy Rates

Allen, Marcus T., Ronald C. Rutherford, and Larry J. Warner, "A Comparison of Federal Government Office Rents with Market Rents." *The Journal of Real Estate Finance and Economics* (October 1997): 181-192.

Barnes, K. A. "Rental Concessions and Value." *The Appraisal Journal* (Spring 1986): 167-176.

Building Owners and Managers Association International. *2006 BOMA Experience Exchange Report: Commercial Real Estate's Benchmark for Income and Expense Data.*

Chen, Jun, Ruijue Peng, and Susan Hudson-Wilson. "Is There Momentum in Office Rental Growth? An Empirical Investigation and Test for Space Market Efficiency." *Journal of Real Estate Practice and Education* (2007): 1-23.

Chesler, Alan. "Decision Criteria for Office Lease Concessions." *Real Estate Review* (Winter 1992): 17-24.

Christiansen, W. K. S. "The Naming of Office Buildings: A New Rental Component?" *The Appraisal Journal* (April 1984): 230-236.

Clark, David L., and Charles G. Dannis. "Forecasting Office Rental Rates: Neoclassical Support for Change." *The Appraisal Journal* (January 1992): 113-128.

Dreyer, J., and Kieran Mathieson. "Ensuring Consistency in the Estimation of Vacancy Rates." *The Appraisal Journal* (April 1995): 209-212.

Glascock, John L., Minbo Kim, and C. F. Sirmans. "An Analysis of Office Market Rents: Parameter Constancy and Unobservable Variables." *The Journal of Real Estate Research* (Fall 1993): 625-637.

Gunnelin, Ake, and Bo Soderberg. "Term Structures in the Office Rental Market in Stockholm." *Journal of Real Estate Finance and Economics* (March-May 2003): 241-252.

Hess, Robert, and Youguo Liang. "Decomposing the Recent Office Market Vacancy Spike." *Real Estate Finance* (April 2003): 12-19.

Mourouzi-Sivitanidou, Rena. "Office Rent Processes: The Case of U.S. Metropolitan Markets." *Real Estate Economics* (Summer 2002): 317-344.

Murtaugh, Christopher D., and D. Albert Daspin. "Negotiating Office Lease Operating Cost Pass-Throughs." *Real Estate Review* (Winter 1994): 62-66.

Öven, V. Atilla, and Dilek Pekdemir. "Office Rent Determinants Utilizing Factor Analysis–A Case Study for Istanbul." *The Journal of Real Estate Finance and Economics* (2006): 51-73.

Senn, M. A. *Commercial Leases.* 2 vols. New York: John Wiley and Sons, 1990.

Shilton, Leon G., and Janet K. Tandy. "The Information Precision of CBD Office Vacancy Rates." *The Journal of Real Estate Research* (Summer 1993): 421-444.

Sivitanides, Petros S. "The Rent Adjustment Process and the Structural Vacancy Rate in the Commercial Real Estate Market." *Journal of Real Estate Research* (1997): 195-209.

Stotler, James. "Estimating the Value of a Leased Fee Estate." *Real Estate Review* (Winter 1995): 41-44.

Vandell, Kerry D., and Jonathan S. Lane. "The Economics of Architecture and Urban Design: Some Preliminary Findings." *Journal of the American Real Estate & Urban Economics Association* (1989): 235-260.

Wheaton, William C., and Raymond G. Torto. "Vacancy Rates and the Future of Office Rents." *Journal of the American Real Estate & Urban Economics Association* (1988): 430-436.

Wincott, D. Richard. "Vacancy Rates and Reasonableness." *The Appraisal Journal* (October 1997): 362-370.

Capitalization Rates

Accetta, Gregory J. "Supporting Capitalization Rates." *The Appraisal Journal* (October 1998): 371-374.

Ambrose, Brent W., and Hugh O. Nourse. "Factors Influencing Capitalization Rates." *The Journal of Real Estate Research* (Spring 1993): 221-237.

Bradley, David M. "The Capitalization Rate, the Discount Rate, and Inflation." *The Appraisal Journal* (April 1989): 237-243.

Devaney, Michael. "Deconstructing Overall Capitalization Rates." *The Appraisal Journal* (Winter 2005): 68-77.

Eppli, Mark J. "The Theory, Assumptions, and Limitations of Direct Capitalization." *The Appraisal Journal* (July 1993): 419-425.

Goeke, D. Michael. "Interrelationship of Variables in the Band-of-Investment Method." *The Appraisal Journal* (April 1991): 261-265.

Honnold, Keith L. "The Link Between Discount Rates and Capitalization Rates: Revisited." *The Appraisal Journal* (April 1990): 190-195.

Jackson, Marcus. "The Gordon Growth Model and the Income Approach to Value." *The Appraisal Journal* (January 1994): 124-128.

Jud, G. Donald, and Daniel T. Winkler. "The Capitalization Rate of Commercial Properties and Market Returns." *The Journal of Real Estate Research* (1995): 509-518.

Kelly, Wayne, Donald R. Epley, and Phillip Mitchell. "A Requiem for Ellwood." *The Appraisal Journal* (July 1995): 284-290.

Kincheloe, Stephen C. "The Weighted Average Cost of Capital: The Correct Discount Rate." *The Appraisal Journal* (January 1990): 88-95.

Ling, D. C., and H. C. Smith. "Linkages Among Capitalization Rates, Discount Rates, and Real Estate Cycles." *Real Estate Issues*, vol. 17, no. 2 (Fall/Winter 1992): 21-26.

Martin, Joseph H., and Mark W. Sussman. "The Twelve *Rs*: An Overview of Capitalization Rate Derivation." *The Appraisal Journal* (April 1997): 149-155.

Owens, Robert W. "An Appraiser Examines Four Types of Return Rates." *Real Estate Review* (Winter 1996): 37-41.

Parker, David R. "Determinants of the Capitalization Rate: A Hierarchical Framework." *The Appraisal Journal* (April 1994): 278-288.

Plattner, Robert. "Income Capitalization Problems." *The Appraisal Journal* (October 1992): 549-555.

Ramsett, David. "Yield Capitalization for Market Analysis." *The Appraisal Journal* (October 1999): 398-404.

Sevelka, Tony. "Where the Overall Cap Rate Meets the Discount Rate." *The Appraisal Journal* (Spring 2004): 135-146.

Sirmans, C.F., G. Stacy Sirmans, and Ben T. Beasley. "Income Property Valuation and the Use of Market Extracted Overall Capitalization Rates." *The Real Estate Appraiser and Analyst.* (Summer 1986): 64-80.

Sivitanidou, Rena, and Petros Sivitanides. "Office Capitalization Rates: Real Estate and Capital Market Influences." *Journal of Real Estate Finance and Economics* (May 1999): 297-310.

Wang, Ko, Terry V. Grissom, and Su Ham Chan. "The Functional Relationship and Use of Going-In and Going-Out Capitalization Rates." *The Journal of Real Estate Research* (Summer 1990): 231-245.

Wincott, D. Richard. "Terminal Capitalization Rates and Reasonableness." *The Appraisal Journal* (April 1991): 253-260.

Discount Rates

Accetta, Gregory J. "Testing the Reasonableness of Discounted Cash Flow Analysis." *The Appraisal Journal* (January 1998): 62-67.

Boice, R. Lane. "Discounted Cash Flow Analysis and Long-Term Leases." *The Appraisal Journal* (April 1999): 153-156.

Gibson, Robert A. "Ellwood is Discounted Cash Flow Before Taxes." *The Appraisal Journal* (July 1986): 406-415.

Ling, David C. "Implementing Discounted Cash Flow Valuation Models: What is the Correct Discount Rate?" *The Appraisal Journal* (April 1992): 267-274.

PricewaterhouseCoopers. *Korpacz Real Estate Investor Survey.* Third Quarter, 2006. vol. 19, no. 13.

Walker, Patrick M. "Establishing Realistic Discount Rates in Unstable Markets." *The Real Estate Appraiser & Analyst* (Winter 1989): 37-42.

Wit, Ivo De, and Ronald Van Dijk. "The Global Determinants of Direct Office Real Estate Returns." *Journal of Real Estate Finance and Economics* (January 2003): 27-35.

Chapter 6. The Sales Comparison Approach

Clapp, John M., Carmelo Giaccotto, and Gregory Richo. "Estimating Time Adjustments with Sales Prices and Assessed Values." *The Appraisal Journal* (July 1996): 319-326.

Clark, D. "Cash Equivalency Adjustments in Depressed Real Estate Markets." *The Appraisal Journal* (October 1989): 544-550.

Kincheloe, Stephen C. "Linear Regression Analysis of Economic Variables in the Sales Comparison and Income Approaches." *The Appraisal Journal* (October 1993): 576-586.

Newsome, Bobby A., and Joachim Zietz. "Adjusting Comparable Sales Using Multiple Regression Analysis: The Need for Segmentation." *The Appraisal Journal* (January 1992): 129-135.

Newsome, L. D. "Financing and Its Influence on Property Valuation." *Appraisal Review Journal*, vol. 2 (1982).

Pardue, William P., Jr. "Checklist for Confirming Sales." *The Appraisal Journal* (April 1986): 274-281.

Pollakowski, Henry O., Susan M. Wachter, and Lloyd Lynford. "Did Office Market Size Matter in the 1980's? A Time-Series Cross-Sectional Analysis of Metropolitan Area Office Markets." *Journal of the American Real Estate and Urban Economics Association* (1992): 303-324.

Ramsland, Maxwell O., Jr., and Daniel E. Markham. "Market-Supported Adjustments Using Multiple Regression Analysis." *The Appraisal Journal* (April 1998): 181-191.

Rattermann, Mark R. "The Market History of the Subject: Analytical Tool or Fourth Approach to Value?" *The Appraisal Journal* (Spring 2005): 175-182.

———. *Valuation by Comparison: Residential Analysis and Logic.* Chicago: Appraisal Institute, 2007.

Shilling, James D., John D. Benjamin, and C. F. Sirmans. "Adjusting Comparable Sales for Floodplain Location." *The Appraisal Journal* (July 1985): 429-436.

Slade, Barrett A. "Conditions of Sale Adjustment: The Influence of Buyer and Seller Motivations on Sale Price." *The Appraisal Journal* (Winter 2004): 50-56.

Williams, Thomas P. "Base Adjusting in the Sales Comparison Approach." *The Appraisal Journal* (Spring 2004): 155-162.

Wincott, D. Richard. "A Primer on Comparable Sale Confirmation." *The Appraisal Journal* (July 2002): 274-282.

Chapter 7. The Cost Approach

Bottum, MacKenzie S. "Estimating Economic Obsolescence in Supply-Saturated Office Markets." *The Appraisal Journal* (October 1988): 451-455.

Jensen, B. R. "Building Efficiency: Cost and Value." *The Appraisal Journal* (January 1985): 127-138.

Laronge, Joseph A. "Solving the Functional Obsolescence Calculation Question?" *The Appraisal Journal* (July 2000): 327-339.

Laronge, Joseph A., and Kerry D. Vandell. "Solving the Functional Obsolescence Calculation Question? Part II." *The Appraisal Journal* (April 2001): 152-160.

Remsett, David E. "The Cost Approach: An Alternative View." *The Appraisal Journal* (April 1998): 172-180.

Sivitanides, Petros S., and Rena C. Sivitanidou. "Construction Movements in Office-Commercial Real Estate Markets." *Real Estate Finance* (Winter 1999): 51-59.

Sivitanidou, Rena, and Petros Sivitanides. "Does the Theory of Irreversible Investments Help Explain Movements in Office-Commercial Construction?" *Real Estate Economics* (2000): 623-661.

Wheaton, William C., and William Eric Simonton. "The Secular and Cyclic Behavior of 'True' Construction Costs." *Journal of Real Estate Research* (January 2006): 1-24.

Wolverton, Marvin L. "Empirical Analysis of the Breakdown Method of Estimating Physical Depreciation." *The Appraisal Journal* (April 1998): 163-171.